The Coniston Railway

by
Robert Western

THE OAKWOOD PRESS

© Oakwood Press & Robert Western 2007

British Library Cataloguing in Publication Data
A Record for this book is available from the British Library
ISBN 978 0 85361 667 2

Typeset by Oakwood Graphics.
Repro by PKmediaworks, Cranborne, Dorset.
Printed by Cambrian Printers, Aberystwyth, Ceredigion.

By the same author

The Ingleton Branch, Oakwood Press, 1990 (first published as *The Lowgill Branch*, The Oakwood Press, 1971).
The Eden Valley Railway, The Oakwood Press, 1997.
The Cockermouth, Keswick and Penrith Railway, The Oakwood Press, 2001 (reprinted 2007).

A third class ticket for the Furness Rail Circular Tour No. 1. The left side is coloured bright pink, the right side is buff.

Rear cover, upper: A first class ticket for the Furness Rail Circular Tour No. 1. The left side is coloured yellow, the right side is buff.

Rear cover, lower: A first class ticket for the Furness Rail Circular Tour No. 2. The ticket is buff with a horizontal yellow band acroos the centre.

Cover: Travel in 1910, Coniston steam motor train, Furness Railway by C. Hamilton Ellis reproduced from an original carriage print.   *Author's Collection*

Published by The Oakwood Press (Usk), P.O. Box 13, Usk, Mon., NP15 1YS.
E-mail: sales@oakwoodpress.co.uk
Website: www.oakwoodpress.co.uk

Contents

A commercial postcard of *Gondola* on Lake Coniston postmarked 1922.

Author's Collection

This map shows the situation in 1852. It was included in *A Handbook of The Whitehaven and Furness Railway, Being a Guide to the Lake District of West Cumberland and Furness* by John Linton. Linton informs us that at this time 200-300 tons of copper ore were being extracted at Coniston each month and these contained on average 11-12 per cent copper, varying in price from £6 to £13 per ton and that about 500 men were employed at the mines.

Chapter One

Beginnings, The Romans to 1856

There are many, whether resident in the Lake District or visitors, who claim Lake Coniston to be their favourite of all the lakes. It retains a serenity and a special quality of calm. A visit in the early morning in September, when the mist is rising gently above the mirror surface of the water, works a special sort of magic. Coniston, with its beauty, might well have been the obvious destination for a railway; a railway to provide access, not least, for visitors to come and enjoy this special area of the Lake District. Access to Windermere and Lake Windermere was made possible when a branch line opened in 1847 from the main line at Oxenholme. Then why not Coniston as a suitable candidate for a similar link as more and more people sought to enjoy the tranquillity of this scenic part of Britain? Certainly Coniston did get a railway but providing a facility for visitors was not the primary reason for building it. Industrial commerce was the driving force, not tourism. And it was copper which was a prime, if not the only, consideration.

Copper, together with its close cousins, silver and gold, has been prized for centuries. To a large degree they have been used for ornamental work but copper, with its more durable qualities, has also been used for utensils. The Romans discovered and mined copper during their sojourn in Cumberland. In later years, during the 16th century, the extraction of copper became a growing industry. Although copper was being produced in the Keswick area in 1565, during the reign of Elizabeth I, the discovery of a rich copper deposit near Newlands, also near Keswick, led to increased production with both mining and smelting being carried out in the locality. During the Civil War the Cumberland mines were destroyed. Yet this was not the end. Copper was still in demand. The monopoly created by the Mines Royal was done away with in 1689 following the passing of the Mines Royal Act and this opened the way for private enterprise. In the latter part of the 18th century the demand for copper escalated. Not only did this demand increase markedly for items such as coinage, buckles, buttons, toys and brass goods, together with a greater call for elaborate brass ornamentation for items such as carriages and furniture, but the introduction of steam power and other industrial developments demanded more and more copper. Brass cylinders were needed and with them a very wide variety of brass fittings. Later still, the introduction of the telegraph in the mid-nineteenth century sent the demand for copper soaring higher still, as its excellent conduction properties resulted in it being very much in demand for a wide variety of applications. At the end of the 18th century, Britain was the world leader in the production of copper and although this would soon change with discoveries in the 'New World' and Chile, in the middle of the 19th century, there was still a considerable market and profit to be made from this valuable commodity. And there was copper at Coniston.

The scheme to build a railway to Coniston was one which rode on the back of other railway schemes, in particular, the Furness Railway. This railway was also

Advertisements from Linton's guide of 1852. By this time the Coniston Waterhead hotel has passed into the ownership of T. Atkinson.

born of an industrial womb. Lord Burlington (later to become the Fourth Duke of Devonshire) owned lands on which there were iron ore and slate. The demand for the former rose with the demand for iron and then steel. Together with this, the rapid surge in house building which took place during the 19th century needed slate in greater and greater quantities. Getting the iron ore and slate out to a wide market from what was a remote area of West Cumberland and Lancashire (on the northern side of Morecambe Bay) was not proving easy. The commodities had to be brought to the coast for shipment and what was needed was an effective form of land transport. A railway was the answer. Such a system had been well tried in areas such as Northumberland, Durham, Derbyshire and Nottinghamshire to move coal from the collieries down to the rivers and canals and here was a pressing opportunity to apply the idea to move the iron ore and slate. A line planned in 1846 to do this might well have been operated by horse-drawn waggons but there was a better form of power in the offing; the steam locomotive was in the ascendancy.

Following the necessary Parliamentary procedures, a line was built which facilitated access for shipment. The system was soon expanded and eventually a further section of railway built to Broughton-in-Furness. Meanwhile, The Whitehaven & Furness Junction Railway was in the process of building a line from Whitehaven to a junction on the Furness near Foxfield with resulting access to Broughton. Once these schemes were completed, a logical development would be to build a line from Broughton up to Coniston, as this would enable the copper ore from Coniston to be moved out more easily. The arrangement at the time was to bring the ore down to Lake Coniston in horse-drawn carts and sledges, then transport it down the lake by barge and finally take it on another journey overland to Broughton. However, neither the Furness Railway nor the Whitehaven & Furness Junction Railway seemed disposed to make a move to develop a branch to Coniston. The travelling public had the use of 'omnibuses' (the contemporary parlance for horse-drawn conveyances) linking Coniston to Broughton and in 1848 it was possible to travel from here to catch a Fleetwood steamer and so onwards to, say, London. The journey to the capital could take as much as 12 hours and there was very little choice as far as times were concerned. In October 1848 J.G. Marshall, who owned the inn at Coniston Waterhead, may have heard that something was afoot which might result in an increase in visitors to Coniston. He decided to take down the inn and 'erect' what was described as 'a handsome hotel with ornamental grounds which would have a good view of the lake'.

The Whitehaven & Furness Junction Railway opened for public traffic between Whitehaven and Ravenglass on Thursday 19th July, 1849 and was at Broughton by October 1850. Meanwhile, on 15th November, 1849, a notice appeared in *Soulby's Ulverstone Advertiser*. It is headed simply 'Broughton-in-Furness and Coniston Railway'. It was issued by William Currey and J.P. Myers, solicitors. It begins:

Notice is hereby given that application is intended to be made to Parliament in the ensuing Session for an Act to authorize the construction and maintenance of a Railway or Railways with all proper Works, Stations, Approaches and Conveniences connected therewith, commencing at the Station or Terminus of the Broughton Branch of the

Furness Railway at Broughton-in-Furness in the Parish of Kirkby Ireleth, in the County of Lancaster and terminating in a field called 'The Field behind the Forge' or 'The New Field' whereof James Wood and John Steel are the owners, and George Dodgson an occupier in the Township of Coniston, in the Parish of Ulverston.

The notice goes on to describe how the Act will enable the alteration of tramways, turnpike roads, canals and assorted other things for the purpose of building the line. Further, that all the maps, plans and sections together with the Book of Reference would be deposited on or before 13th November with the Clerk of the Peace for the County of Lancaster at his Office in Preston and with the appropriate Parish Clerks.

Progress at last. J.G. Marshall might well have felt satisfied with his plans to provide more and better accommodation, except that he had decided to move to Headingly. The new hotel opened the same month with an auspicious opening ceremony, which included a grand fireworks display. As far as the plan for the line was concerned, nothing further happened. No notice appeared in the *London Gazette* or, for that matter, the *Railway Record*. It would seem unlikely that any plans or scheme were sent to Preston. There was certainly no Bill and therefore no Act. All the documentation, if there actually was any (although it is hard to believe, given the projected timings that there wasn't) seems to have disappeared without trace. Further, the newspaper in which the notice appeared did not carry a story associated with it; surprising, when many local people would no doubt see it as a significant development. Then again, the *Advertiser*, a small newspaper, had the responsibility of bringing the good people of Ulverston the international as well as national news, not to mention the reporting of 'terrible murders' and 'executions' which, possibly, the readers found more to their liking than the news of the proposal to build a short length of railway line.

The reason for abandoning the plan is not really clear. According to notes made by W.B. Kendall, who was associated with the Furness Railway (FR) and who gives what is virtually a contemporary account, the railway, planned by Barraclough, would not have been standard gauge and that fact may have given rise to some misgivings by the Earl of Burlington, who was Chairman of the FR. Cost may have also been an issue. Whatever the reason or reasons, Coniston had to wait a little longer for a rail connection. In the event, all was not lost. Seven years later, almost to the day (this time 20th November) another notice appeared in the *Advertiser*. On this occasion the heading is simply 'Coniston Railway'. However, this did not happen before a good deal of talking and planning had taken place.

Another important local industry which would benefit from a railway link from Coniston onto the national system, was the slate industry. Coniston slate was much sought after in this period because it was valued for its blue and green hues, which slate coming from the Cavendish quarries lacked. Even so, it would seem it was those whose main interests were in copper who were ready to provide capital to enable the building of a rail link.

Chapter Two

Setting up the Company and Building the Line, 1856-1859

The Le Flemings had been in Coniston for several centuries and Dame Anne Frederica Elizabeth Le Fleming, Lady of the Manor of Coniston, owned 'extensive copper mines in the neighbourhood of Coniston'. (She had also owned slate mines.) The copper mines were leased by John Barratt, James Humbleton and Joseph Mason. Getting the copper out of Coniston to meet the needs of an ever growing market was becoming more and more a pressing issue. Although there had been improvements to the road, access was still difficult. However, the Furness Railway had reached Broughton and it was but eight miles from there to Coniston. The proposals of 1849 had come to nought but the prospect of a rail link was still one to be encouraged and so Dame Anne agreed (probably after some encouragement) to purchase £4,000 worth of shares in relation to the capital required for a scheme. Her lessees were equally keen and between them offered to purchase a further £6,000 worth of shares, giving a total of £10,000 worth in all; no mean sum. What is more we are told they were 'content' to receive a fixed dividend of £2 10s. on these shares because 'the Railway would be of great Advantage to them'. The decision had been prompted by the Furness Railway which it soon became clear was influencing events in the background. On the other hand, the fact that this group would be purchasing shares for nearly 25 per cent of the total capital needed would seem to be an indication of the real *raison d'etre* for building the line. There were others keen to be a part of this new venture: His Grace the Duke of Buccleuch, the Right Honorable the Earl of Burlington, James Walker, Frederick Iltid Nicholl, Stephen Eddy, Frederick Currey, William Currey and James Ramsden. It was not without significance that there was a strong Furness flavour here.

The intention to place a Bill before Parliament was made known in 1856. Notice was given that this would be no later than 29th November.

The Line

The route had been surveyed by George Saunders and the plans drawn up by Messrs McClean and Stileman.

The line would run for a distance of 8 miles and 60 chains. It would be standard gauge and was to be single throughout with sidings only at the stations. There was no intention to double the line and therefore no provision was made, even in the planning stage, for this type of development. Twenty-one bridges were planned on the line with eight of these being overbridges. The bridges would be built of stone, stone and brick or stone abutments with timber tops. There would be one exception. One of the underbridges would have stone abutments and cast-iron girders, 22 ft on the skew. The greatest span of an overbridge would be 24 ft on the square. There would be one viaduct having five arches of 28 ft span.

ANNO VICESIMO & VICESIMO PRIMO

VICTORIÆ REGINÆ.

****

Cap. cx.

An Act for making a Railway from *Broughton* to
Coniston in the County Palatine of *Lancaster;*
and for other Purposes.   [10th *August* 1857.]

WHEREAS the Construction of a Railway from the Terminus of the *Furness* Railway at *Broughton* in the County
Palatine of *Lancaster* to *Coniston* in the same County
would be of great public Advantage : And whereas the Persons herein-
after named, together with other Persons, are willing at their own
Expense to carry such Undertaking into execution if authorized so to
do : And whereas it is expedient that the *Furness* Railway Company
should be authorized to subscribe towards and become Shareholders in
the Undertaking, and to give such Guarantees as are herein-after
mentioned in respect of the Dividend on a Portion of the Capital
required for the Construction of the said proposed Railway : And
whereas the several Matters aforesaid cannot be effected without the
Authority of Parliament : May it therefore please Your Majesty that
it may be enacted ; and be it enacted by the Queen's most Excellent
Majesty, by and with the Advice and Consent of the Lords Spiritual
and Temporal, and Commons, in this present Parliament assembled,
and by the Authority of the same, as follows ; (that is to say,)

[*Local.*]   18 *N*   I. " The

The title page of the Act to build the Coniston Railway.

1857

On 9th February, a Deed of Agreement between the promoters of the Coniston Railway, the Furness Railway and the owners and lessees of the Coniston Copper Mines was considered by the Directors who raised no objections although the matter of the £10,000 input by the last of these groups was a matter referred over to a meeting when the Chairman could be present. However, it was acknowledged that the duration of the toll agreed to be paid by Lady Le Fleming and her lessees between the Furness Railway and for working the Coniston Railway by the Furness Railway should be settled before the passing of the Act.

The Act for the building of the Coniston Railway (CR) was placed on the Statute Book on 10th August, 1857. It is entitled 'An Act for making a Railway from Broughton to Coniston in the County Palatine of Lancaster and for other purposes'. Although the company to be set up was an independent one (the Coniston Railway Company) the Furness Railway is referred to in the Act at least 17 times. The direction in which events would move later might well have been predictable. The first Directors of the company, which were to number three, each holding at least 50 shares, are named as Messrs Nicholl, Eddy and (Frederick) Currey. They were given the usual proviso, namely of holding office until the first shareholders' meeting when they would in effect stand down and elections take place. All were eligible for re-election. The capital for the company was set at £45,000 with provision for 4,500 £10 shares. However, as indicated earlier, some of these shares were already spoken for.

Provision was also made in the Act for the extension of the line, beyond that shown on the deposited plan, for the purpose of laying down a mineral line. This would service the copper mines. There was a further section dealing with the matter of level crossings. The company is instructed that where the line crosses a road on the same level, it must construct a lodge or station. Five such crossings are referred to. It was further laid down in the Act the dimensions of the bridges it must build.

The first General Meeting of the company, following the Act, took place on 27th August at the Waterhead Inn, Coniston. The minutes of the General Meetings and also the Directors' Meetings are minimal, to say the least, with little detail given for posterity. The handwriting also leaves much to be desired and there are places where the words are virtually illegible. The first meeting was attended by the Earl of Burlington, Mr Eddy, Mr Nicholl, Mr William Currey, Mr Ramsden and one other. Mr Nicholl was in the chair. The register book of shareholders was produced (we are told) and the seal of the company ordered to be affixed. The Earl of Burlington was elected a Director in place of Mr Frederick Currey, who had resigned, and Messrs Eddy and Nicholl were re-elected as Directors. So ended the meeting. On the same day the Directors met. The venue was the same as the General Meeting and therefore it would follow that the two meetings were held consecutively. The Directors meeting was attended by the Earl of Burlington (who was elected Chairman), Mr Nicholl and Mr Eddy. Mr Ramsden was appointed Secretary. Messrs McClean and Stileman were confirmed as the Engineers, Mr William Currey became the solicitor and

20° & 21° VICTORIÆ, *Cap*.cx.   1615

The Coniston Railway Act, 1857.

VII. Whereas Dame *Anne Frederica Elizabeth Le Fleming* is Lady of the Manor of *Coniston* and the Owner of extensive Mines of Copper in the Neighbourhood thereof, and *John Barratt, James Humbleton,* and *Joseph Mason* are the Lessees of the Mines, and the proposed Railway will take Traffic to and from the Mines : And whereas, for the Purpose of facilitating the making the Railway, Lady *Anne Frederica Elizabeth Le Fleming* has subscribed for Shares to the Amount of Four thousand Pounds in the Capital of the Company, and *John Barratt, James Humbleton,* and *Joseph Mason* have also subscribed for Shares to the Amount of Six thousand Pounds therein, and they respectively are content to receive a fixed Dividend at the Rate of Two Pounds Ten Shillings on the Sums from Time to Time paid on those Shares respectively : And whereas the *Furness* Railway Company are of opinion that the Construction of the Railway would be of great Advantage to them, and are therefore willing to incur the Liability with respect to the Dividends to be paid on the Shares so subscribed for which is imposed on them by this Act : Therefore the Holders of the Shares so subscribed for, and amounting together to Ten thousand Pounds, shall not be entitled to any Dividend out of the Profits of the Company exceeding the Rate of Two Pounds Ten Shillings *per Centum per Annum* on the Amount from Time to Time paid on those Shares ; and if and whenever the Company do not for any Half Year declare and pay a Dividend at the Rate of One Pound Five Shillings *per Centum* on the Amount so paid up, the *Furness* Railway Company shall, in priority to any Dividend for that Half Year on the ordinary Shares in their Capital, and to any Dividend for that Half Year on any preferential Shares in their Capital, created or issued by them after the passing of this Act, but not in priority to any Dividend on any preferential Shares in their Capital created or issued by them before the passing of this Act, pay to the Holders of those Shares such a Sum as is sufficient to make the Dividend thereon for that Half Year equal to One Pound Five Shillings *per Centum :* Provided always, that the Company shall issue the Certificates for those Shares on such Terms as shall sufficiently indicate the special Provisions of this Act with respect to the Dividends to be paid thereon.

Marginal note: Dividend to be paid on Shares for 10,000*l*. subscribed for by Owner and Lessees of Coniston Copper Mines.

Clause VII in the Act to build the Coniston Railway which refers to copper interests.

Messrs Dixon & Company of Chancery Lane, London together with the Lancaster Banking Company were appointed bankers. It was agreed that cheques must be signed either by the Chairman or two Directors and countersigned by the Secretary. The Engineers were instructed to complete the further surveys, prepare estimates and obtain tenders ready for the next meeting. In addition, the Secretary and the solicitor were to take the necessary steps for giving legal effects to the agreements already entered into for the purchase of land and to negotiate for the purchase of such land as had already been contracted for. These meetings over, the initial steps for the actual building of the line had been taken.

The next Directors' meeting took place on 17th November, this time at 9 Old Burlington Street in London. The same Directors were present as before, with the Secretary, the solicitor and Mr Stileman. It was resolved that a call of £2 10s. per share should be made on the capital of the company on the 15th December. The next matter to be addressed was that involving tenders. For the purpose of submitting tenders the line had been divided into three sections. Ten tenders had been submitted although two were tenders for Section 3 only. The spread in projected costs was considerable. At the top end there was a figure of £41,180 14s. 6d. and at the bottom end (excluding the two part-tenders) £19,779 11s. 2d. The projected time for construction also varied considerably. One contractor gave the completion date as early as 31st July, 1858, another as late as December 1859. There is no correlation between 'cost' and 'projected time', one of the cheapest estimates being linked to one of the shortest times. The Engineers' estimate had been £23,370 13s. 7d. with a completion date of 1st May, 1859. With this in view the contract was awarded to Child & Pickles. They had given a price of £20,907 11s. 8d. (Section 1 £7,591 18s. 4½d., Section 2 £7,572 15s. 3½d. and Section 3 £5,743 5s. 9½d.) and a completion date of March 1859. There was only one tender lower than this.

1858

The next minuted General Meeting was held on 26th August, 1858. On this occasion it was held in Barrow. The Duke of Devonshire (formerly the Earl of Burlington) was in the chair and the Secretary did not deem it necessary to make a note of those present! In what appears to be a remarkably brief meeting (if the minutes are anything to go by) Mr Walker proposed and Mr Nicholl seconded that the seal be applied to the register of shareholders. The Chairman proposed and Mr Eddy seconded that the report be accepted and circulated. Finally Mr Walker proposed and Mr Eddy seconded a vote of thanks to the Chairman. And that was that. This basic pattern is repeated a number of times.

1859

A Directors' meeting was held at 9 Old Burlington Street on 16th February, 1859. The half-yearly report for the shareholders was approved for the meeting on the 25th February and then the Engineers were instructed to prepare drawings and obtain tenders for the construction of station buildings at Coniston and Torver and also for the gate keepers' lodges at 'the public surface crossings'. These drawings and tenders were to be submitted to the Chairman and it was agreed that he should authorize the work being done if he approved what he was given.

At the General Meeting on 26th February in 9 Old Burlington Street, there was an additional matter. The terms proposed for a working agreement with the FR were considered and agreed in principle. The solicitor was instructed to prepare a full working agreement.

The second half-yearly meeting of the Directors was held on 24th August, again at No. 9 with the business, once more, being minimal.

The acquisition of plots of land by compulsory purchase for the purpose of building railways often proved to be a contentious issue. There were usually those who welcomed the coming of a railway and, as a result, were ready to accept what they felt to be a fair price from the company building the line. However, there were also those who had no particular interest in seeing a railway built and so opposed the sale of land whatever the price. Those who found themselves (usually individuals rather than trusts, for example) owning land which the railway needed, would be asked whether they would 'assent' or 'dissent'. In the early days, especially, when this whole business was a new experience, rumour and, indeed, some malpractices were quite commonplace. There were those who found that somehow they had 'dissented' when they had said they wished to assent; and vice-versa. (The promoters of the Eden Valley Railway had considerable problems with cases of this sort of chicanery.) There are occasions where a story was put around that those who did not assent would almost certainly end up, eventually, getting a lower price for their land from the railway company than had been originally offered. There are cases where schemes were held up whilst claims went to lengthy arbitration.

As far as The Coniston Railway was concerned, there was at least one long-running dispute. This involved Mr John Sawrey of Broughton Tower. John Sawrey, a wealthy landowner, had shown an interest in railway development and this interest included the South Durham & Lancashire Union Railway. The Coniston Railway Company would need land from his estate. He did not appear to object to this in principle but he certainly objected to the sum on offer. The correspondence is legion and a considerable number of individuals were involved at various stages. The letters appear to commence in April 1857, when Job Bintley wrote to John Sawrey to say he would look over the property 'which the railway intends to take'. Some of the letters which follow are written on the flimsiest of notepaper (akin to tracing paper) and much of the writing is faded and sometimes illegible. Several of the letters are undated. In essence, the amount of money being offered, namely £2,000, was quite unacceptable to Sawrey. Later, Henry Clerkson, writing on behalf of Sawrey, suggests that

Child & Pickles have been overpaid and so, presumably, this is why the amount being offered for land purchase is so low. The correspondence continues to flow until 1862. During the course of this, a claim is filed for £7,000, and what are claimed to be ambiguous offers are made, ranging from £3,461 to £4,970 to £6,525. A London land agent (George Powell) becomes involved; there is disagreement at one stage as to who should be the umpire (arbiter); the Board of Trade is drawn in; a number of local and London solicitors act at various times. At least 30 letters are still extant. In the end the problem was resolved and the railway obtained the land. Even so, the correspondence did not cease because wrangling started involving the fees to be paid for the (legal) work. This, however, was not a concern for the Coniston Railway Company!

Interest in the railway can be found much further afield than the local area. In 1861, James Hambleton who lived in Alstonefield in Staffordshire left 25 shares in the Coniston Railway (together with two in the Coniston copper mines) in trust to William Hambleton, his son, for the benefit of members of his family:

> I, James Hambleton of Alstonefield, in the county of Stafford give and bequeath those my two Shares of and in the Coniston Copper mine situate and being at Coniston in the County Palatine of Lancaster together with those my Twenty-five shares of and in the Railway connected with such Mine and called the Coniston Railway or by whatsoever other name or names the same is or are respectively designated together also with the interest, dividends and proceeds of the same unto my Son William Hambleton his executors and administrators In trust for himself, my said son William my Son George Hambleton and my two daughters Ellen the wife of Thomas Johnson and Eliza Hambleton absolutely share and share alike …

The Level Crossing at Broughton

Shortly after the work started, a memorial (petition) was submitted in connection with the plan to make a level crossing over one of the roads just to the east of Broughton. A group of individuals felt such a crossing was undesirable, not least on safety grounds, and asked that the company be obliged to make a bridge. Concern was expressed in a number of quarters that this proposal had come rather late in the day and, in addition, a counter memorial was sent to the Lords. It begins as follows:

> To the Right Honourable the Lords of the Committee of Her Majesty's Privy Council for Trade … That your memorialists have been informed that a petition has recently been presented to your Lordships requesting your interference to compel the erection by the Coniston Railway Company of a bridge over the line of the said railway in the Town of Broughton and that such a petition represents that the safety of the Public will be endangered if the said Company are allowed to construct a level crossing …

The 'memorialists' go on to point out that in their view such a bridge is unnecessary. It will, they claim, impose a great expense on the railway company and, perhaps more to the point, would 'render necessary the destruction of a considerable extent of cottage property' This action would, it was said, cause great inconvenience to both owners and occupiers. The petitioners make it very clear that they wish to see the railway built, indeed (magnanimously) they do not want the building of it presented with any 'obstacles' and that includes the need to build a bridge. The memorial carries 65 signatures and those placing their names to it come from a wide variety of backgrounds. There are farmers, those who describe themselves as yeomen, a mechanic, a butcher, a group of gentlemen, a solicitor, some who style themselves simply with the title 'esquire', a tailor, shop-keepers, a wood dealer, a hotel keeper, a blacksmith, a clock and watch-maker, a retired clergyman, a shoe maker, a wood dealer, a surgeon, a painter and a plate-layer. Clearly the railway was supported by a very wide section of the community living in Broughton.

This material was passed on to Colonel Yolland at the Board of Trade. He was instructed to pay a visit to Broughton to find out first-hand what the matter was all about. Following his visit he produced a report. It is lengthy, although not written in his own hand, as many were, but only signed by him. During the visit he inspected the site and met Mr Noble Jackson, the Surveyor of Highways. In addition he spoke with several residents, the incumbent of the chapelry, the Engineer and the Secretary of the Coniston Railway.

In the report, Colonel Yolland indicates where the crossing is and the fact that work has already begun in the vicinity with rails 'roughly laid'. He points out that there are two roads only 30 yards apart where the level crossing is planned and that the company has the power to divert the southern road and carry the railway across the northern road 'on the level'. He then discloses that when the railway was projected, three alternative lines were presented to the Lord of the Manor who chose the one submitted to Parliament:

> ... and it is certain that another line might have been taken which would have done away with the necessity for the crossing of the road on a level and even along the present line this might have been affected by carrying the railway at the lower level and under the road but this would have been at considerable increased cost to the company for the construction of an overbridge and compensation to the owners of adjoining property...

The Colonel indicated that he had found very differing views among the residents about the crossing and he adds a note in his own hand to the document about what he refers to as the counter memorial. The Reverend Robinson (who did not sign the memorial) entirely disapproved of a bridge because 'it would have the effect of entirely burying' his house. Arguments were also presented concerning the amount of traffic passing over the roads with the view that the southern road carried the most. The amount of traffic over the other road, whilst considerable, was of a type, Yolland felt, which would reduce once the railway was open. There were no public conveyances 'save a mail cart which did not carry passengers'. Someone had gone to the trouble of carrying out a traffic census relating to how many vehicles might use the crossing. It only covered four days! On the first, 21 carts, on the second 19 carts, on the third 15 carts and on the fifth, 17 carts. (Presumably these dates refer to April and the fourth was a Sunday.) After looking at the evidence Colonel Yolland came to the following conclusion:

I do not think this is a case where their Lordships should call upon the Railway Company to construct a bridge but I do think it very desirable that the level crossing should be constructed at No. 43, the Southern instead of the Northern Road (No. 44 as sanctioned by the Company's Act) as approach to it is better and safer ... and I beg therefore that their Lordships should issue their certificate in writing when it is applied for by the Railway Company under the 66th section of the 8th Vic Cap 20 authorizing the construction of the level crossing at No. 43 instead of No. 44 as sanctioned by the Company Special Act.

The date of this document is 14th April, 1858. An additional note on the bottom reads,

We had better transmit a copy of this to the Company and suggest that they should construct their Level Crossing at the road indicated by Colonel Yolland instead of at the place where they are constructing it.

D.Gatton

A further note indicates this was actioned on 19th April, 1859.

On Friday, 25th February, the third half-yearly meeting of the company took place at 9 Old Burlington Street, London. The Engineers' report contained something of a bombshell. Whether the Directors had prior warning is not clear but it was announced that the contractors had gone bankrupt. In view of this, the Engineers had made the decision to oversee the works 'under more immediate supervision'. It was possible to report that since September, 3¼ miles of permanent way had been laid down. Further that no separate work of any great extent remained to be executed. This observation is curious in the light of what the inspector would report some time later and may well have been open to misunderstanding. It was anticipated that the line would be ready for public traffic in the ensuing summer. What was needed next, the Engineers pointed out, was the instruction to prepare drawings and obtain tenders for the construction of station buildings at Coniston and Torver and for the gate keeper's lodge at the public level crossings.

Expenditure at this stage (to 31st December, 1858) was as follows,

	£	s.	d.
Law and Parliamentary Expenses	1,610	5	8
Engineers and Surveying	1,054	13	2
Land and Compensation	5,374	6	8
Rails, chairs, turntables etc.	6,030	7	4
Miscellaneous	140	10	0
'Cash'	595	15	3

At this meeting the Directors considered the terms for the proposed working of the CR by the FR. Coincidentally with the meeting of the CR, the Directors of the FR were also meeting and amongst other things discussed these proposals. It was noted that the expenditure on the Coniston Railway was expected to be £50,000 and the FR would take £10,000 worth of shares. It was proposed that subject to the approval of the Board of Trade the FR would work the line for 10 years and provide all the stock for working the line and take the whole of the receipts and pay all the expenses. There was a slight anomaly in the wording of the agreement when it was stated:

> ... the Furness Railway shall for the first year of this term pay the working expenses and the interest on the debentures and the preference shares and that for the second and third years of the term the Furness Railway shall pay to the holders of the ordinary shares in the Coniston Railway a dividend equal to one third of the dividend paid during that period upon the Ordinary shares of the Furness Railway and the fourth and fifth year a dividend equal to one half of the dividend paid during those years upon the Ordinary shares of the Furness Railway.

The Board of Trade felt there was an implication here that the FR would not be paying any interest except for the first year. Correspondence ensued and in a letter of 8th June alternatives were suggested (and later implemented) to clarify this matter. On 27th June it was possible to conclude that 'The Agreement now sent appears to be in accordance with the terms set out in the reports.... and the Lords are satisfied with the proposals'. The FR would, before long, exercise a much greater influence on this railway.

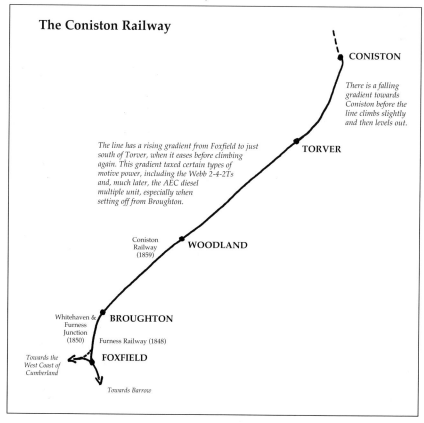

The Coniston Railway

CONISTON

There is a falling gradient towards Coniston before the line climbs slightly and then levels out.

The line has a rising gradient from Foxfield to just south of Torver, when it eases before climbing again. This gradient taxed certain types of motive power, including the Webb 2-4-2Ts and, much later, the AEC diesel multiple unit, especially when setting off from Broughton.

TORVER

Coniston
Railway
(1859)

WOODLAND

Whitehaven &
Furness
Junction
(1850)

BROUGHTON

Furness Railway (1848)

*Towards the
West Coast of
Cumberland*

FOXFIELD

Towards Barrow

Chapter Three

The Opening, Brief Independence,
then the Take Over, 1859-1923

Colonel Yolland Returns, the First Inspection

Following the visit to sort out the dispute about the level crossing, Colonel Yolland returned to Coniston on 25th May, 1859. His purpose on this occasion was to inspect the line in order to ascertain whether or not he could recommend it should be opened. He wrote his report (this time in his own hand) the following day. The report opens with a description of the line and the details of the mode of construction. Double T rails were used, weighing 60 lb. to the yard, with lengths of 18½ ft fixed into ordinary cast-iron chairs, each weighing 20 lb., by 6 in. oak keys. These chairs were fixed to the sleepers which were Larch, 9 in. long and 10 in. by 15 in. laid transversely 3 ft 3 in. apart, except at the joints where they were 2 ft 2 in. apart, using two wrought-iron spikes. The joints were fixed with two fish plates bolted together by four wrought-iron screwed bolts and nuts.

The Colonel took the Engineers' word for the information that the ballast was 2 ft deep, with the lower layer of 12 in. broken stone, the upper being sand and gravel. When it came to the construction, the masonry work was described as 'good' with 'the whole of the bridges sufficiently strong'. There was special mention for the viaduct consisting of five arches of 28 ft span with the observation that 'it is well constructed and amply strong'. So far, so good. The inspector then turned his attention to some other aspects where certain elements were found wanting. He pointed out that:

> ... at Broughton Station, a distant signal is required on the Furness line and the distant signal now on the up Coniston line but not in working order must be used as a repeating signal and another signal erected at a greater distance from the station. The handles of the levers for working the three signals be brought together on the platform.

He notes that the station buildings at Woodland station have just been commenced but that they were scarcely in hand at Torver and Coniston. Further, that the platforms and signal arrangements were incomplete at all three and that the distant signals planned must be placed at greater distances than proposed. There were other reservations. The gates at the level crossings had not been erected and the same applied to the lodges. Considerable sections of fencing still had to be built, for example, at Torver station and some of the bridges and the siding at Woodland were incomplete. The arch of the overbridge at 2 miles 6 chains had not yet been turned and three of the other overbridges (2 miles 14 chains, 4 miles 73 chains and 8 miles 40 chains) were incomplete. The turntable at Coniston had not been put in place but he noted that in working the line, the Furness Railway intended to use a turntable at Foxfield Junction. The list goes on. Temporary sidings needed to be removed; the ballast pit must be protected by signals in both directions; a good deal of 'bolting and screwing yet remains to be done'; some lengths of line needed

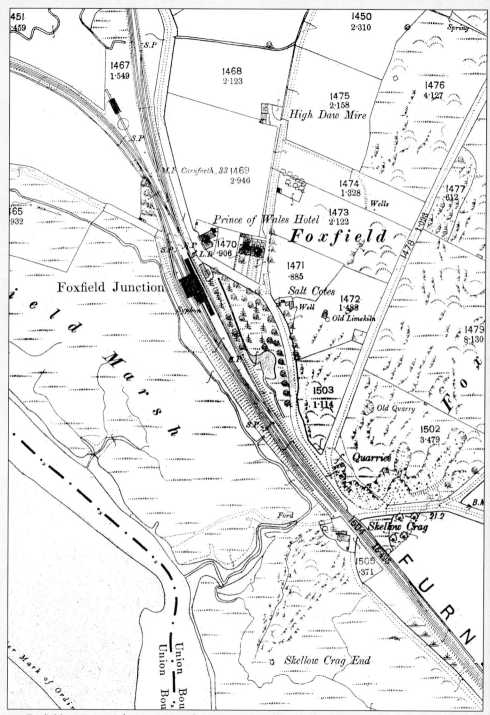

Foxfield station and the junction of the Coniston branch with the main line.
Reproduced from the 25″, 1890 Ordnance Survey Map

A view along the platform at Foxfield looking north towards Workington, 14th September, 1950.
H.C. Casserley

Broughton-in-Furness station looking towards Coniston, 8th August, 1958.   *R.M. Casserley*

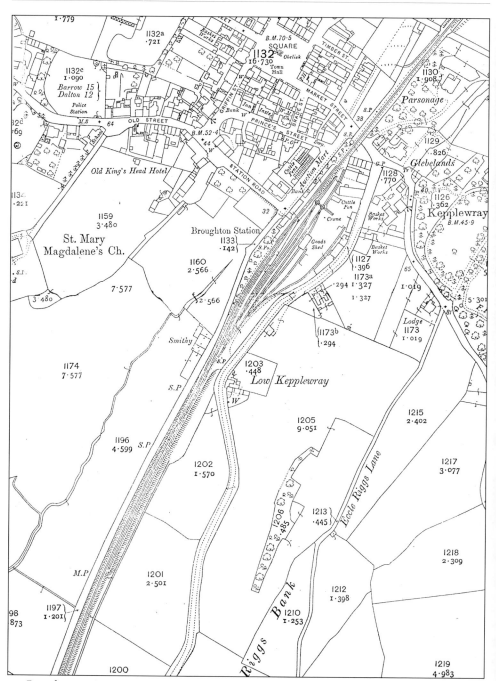

Broughton station.   *Reproduced from the 25", 1913 Ordnance Survey Map*

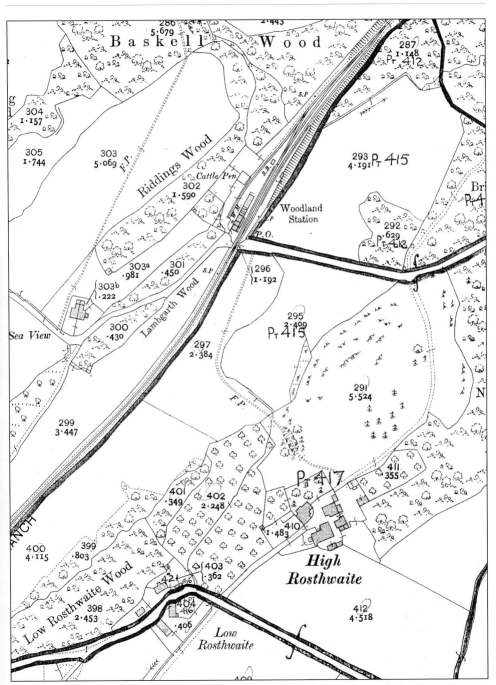

Woodland station.   *Reproduced from the 25", 1913 Ordnance Survey Map*

Woodland Station.

This card, which is lightly tinted, was issued in the early part of the 20th century and is an Illingworth (Millom) card printed in Saxony. It was quite customary to produce cards showing stations with the staff posing on the platform. The card depicts Woodland station, with the post office at the end of the station building. Although this type of card is now very collectable, it is difficult to imagine who would buy such a card (other than members of the station staff and their families, perhaps) when it was first published.   *Author's Collection*

Woodland station viewed from a train looking towards Foxfield, 8th August, 1958.

R.M. Casserley

Torver Station. No. 174

An early view of Torver station looking towards Foxfield. *R.M. Casserley Collection*

Torver station viewed from a train looking towards Coniston, 8th August, 1958.

R.M. Casserley

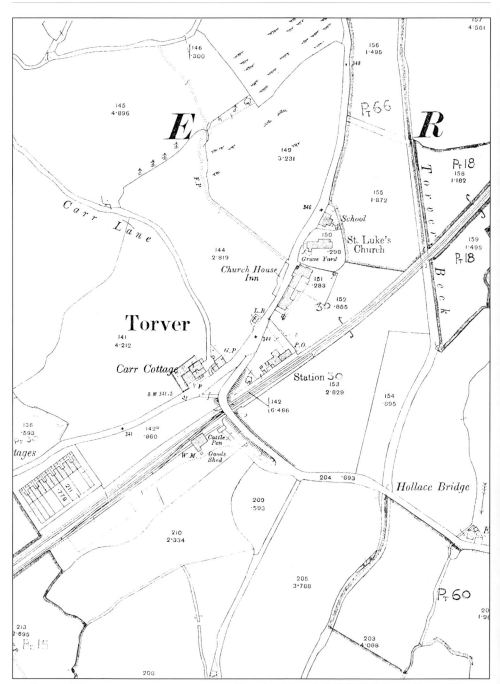

Torver station.   *Reproduced from the 25″, 1914 Ordnance Survey Map*

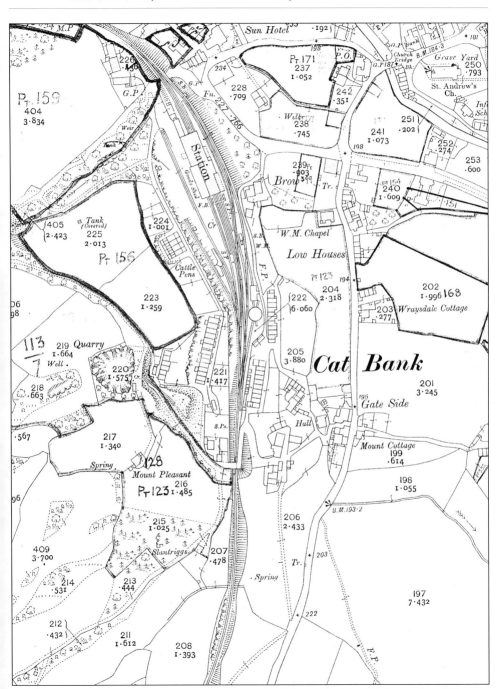

Coniston station.   *Reproduced from the 25", 1913 Ordnance Survey Map*

A fine general view of Coniston station looking north, 24th April, 1960.

P.B. Booth/N. Stead Collection

A view looking towards the train shed at Coniston in the direction of Foxfield, 8th August, 1958.

R.M. Casserley

Coniston station approach, on 5th August, 1958. *R.M. Casserley*

An early view inside the train shed at Coniston looking towards Foxfield.
R.M. Casserley Collection

A view south from Coniston station showing the engine shed and signal box,
R.M. Casserley Collection

Coniston engine shed and turntable looking north, 14th September, 1950.   *H.C. Casserley*

further ballasting; the end of the line must be made secure at Coniston by either buffers or a bank of earth.

At this stage the outcome of the Report was not hard to predict and it must have come as no great surprise to those reading it when it concluded:

> I have therefore to report my opinion that by reason of the incompleteness of the works, the opening of the Coniston Railway for traffic cannot be sanctioned without danger to the Public using the same.

Although this proved something of a set back, it was quite clear that there was a great deal to be done if a reinspection was to recommend the line could open. As a result some acceptable compromises were adopted and Colonel Yolland returned a few weeks later on 14th June. The report this time, again in his own hand, is shorter; in fact, he wrote it on the same day as the inspection. He noted that temporary fencing had been erected where the intention was to put up stone walls and that wooden boxes had been placed at the stations and at the authorized level crossings to serve until the station buildings and lodges were built. The platforms had been finished and the signals erected and were in working order. The arch of the overbridge which had not been commenced on his previous visit had been turned. Other bridges were complete and in use by the public. A buffer had been put up at Coniston:

> I have not received the undertaking as to the manner in which it is proposed to work the line but I am told it will be forwarded to you by the chairman of the Coniston Railway (The Duke of Devonshire) in the course of tomorrow. I understand it is proposed to divide the line into three sections and that the Company will undertake that only one engine in steam or two or more coupled together and forming part of one train shall be upon each section at one time.

Then a proviso:

> Also that the line shall be worked exclusively by tank engines until the turntable at Coniston Station shall be put up, which is expected will be done in less than two months.

Finally another proviso and the section the Directors had hoped would appear:

> If their Lordships are willing to allow the traffic to be worked by tank engines, until the turntable is ready, I see no reason why their consent to the opening of the line be with held provided the Company will engage to remove the facing points leading into the temporary sidings and ballast pit before the opening actually takes place.

This report was acted upon and accepted on 16th June, 1859.

In spite of all this, the people of Coniston had already witnessed the arrival of a locomotive during the evening of Saturday 21st May. Clearly word had gone round that something special was going to happen. The following report appeared in the *Lancaster Guardian* for Saturday 28th May:

> On Saturday evening last, for the first time, the inhabitants of Coniston were gratified by the shrill whistle of the locomotive engine which attracted a large number of people

to Cat Bank to see it pass. We trust the advantages will be neither few nor unimportant that Coniston will derive from the completion of this undertaking. Certainly it will be a boon to the inhabitants of our large manufacturing towns some of whom we hear are to be treated with a sight of the incompatible [*sic*] beauties of Coniston and its neighbourhood, by special train on Whit Monday.

The line opened on 18th June in spite of the fact that the Furness Railway had placed a notice in *Soulby's Ulverston Advertiser* on 2nd June announcing that the opening would be on 8th July. This may have been a misprint because in another part of the same paper 18th June is given as the opening date. A timetable for the line appears in this and subsequent editions. The 'inhabitants of our large manufacturing towns' referred to in the *Guardian's* report were probably disappointed because Whit Monday in 1859 fell on 13th June. The railway company chose not to mark the opening with a special celebration and associated junketings. Even so there were those who were not prepared to see this auspicious moment pass without some recognition. The event is recorded in the *Ulverston Advertiser* of 23rd June, 1859:

> *Broughton and Coniston Railway*
> We have the pleasure to announce that this line was opened for public traffic to Coniston and Coniston Lake on Saturday last. The day was remarkably fine and a large number of visitors took the opportunity of visiting this romantic and beautiful spot in the Lake District. The event was not celebrated by the directors in the mode usually adopted by large companies but the secretary James Ramsden Esq. and Mrs Ramsden entertained a party of friends at the Waterhead Hotel Coniston. The inhabitants of that place, however, were determined not to allow that event to pass off without some little demonstration of feeling and decorated the Coniston station gaily yet tactfully with flags and evergreens and the village itself wore a lively and joyous appearance …

The article goes on to describe places of interest in the area 'for those who may not have visited Coniston'.

On the following Tuesday, 21st June what, in some ways, was a very remarkable excursion took place. Once again this is reported in the *Advertiser*:

> The excursion annually given to the children of the Ulverston National and Town Bank Sunday Schools took place on Tuesday last on which occasion upwards of 430 scholars under the superintendence of their teachers were conveyed by the newly opened line of railroad to Coniston … The great demand for tickets soon filled every carriage at the disposal of the Furness Railway … the train had 30 carriages with upwards of 1,000 persons including many of elite of the neighbourhood …

The visitors were welcomed at Coniston by local people carrying banners 'of peace and goodwill'. Drum and fife accompanied the festivities and the party was entertained in a marquee set up at the Waterhead Hotel, which was run by Mr and Mrs Atkinson 'who were given credit for their excellent arrangements'. Poor weather stopped the afternoon programme of games planned for the children but it was possible to use the marquee and all seem to have had an enjoyable time:

> Omnibuses were in great request as the time of departure approached and the station soon presented the usual scenes of excitement and bustle peculiar to the departure of a

monster train which left at 7 o'clock for Ulverston amid the cheers and good wishes of the inhabitants of Coniston.

What an occasion it must have been. What a pity there is no reference to the motive power used to haul such a 'monster train'.

On normal days with normal services, trains did not run just between Broughton and Coniston; Foxfield Junction was a more appropriate end point for the branch. The timetables which appeared in the local press read (possibly misleading in this respect as they are rather inconsistent but given below as issued) as though most trains ran through to Kirkby-in-Furness. The term 'Down Trains' applied to those leaving Coniston, a scheme which runs counter to the usual convention.

The passenger timetable when the line opened was as follows:

Down Trains	*Weekdays*				*Sundays*	
	am	*am*	*pm*	*pm*	*am*	*pm*
Coniston Lake *(dep.)*	8.00	11.40	2.55	5.45	8.40	5.55
Torver	8.15	11.55	3.10	6.00	8.55	6.10
Woodland	8.30	12.10 *pm*	3.25	6.15	9.10	6.25
Broughton	8.45	12.35	3.40	6.30	9.25	6.40
Foxfield	8.55	12.45	3.45	6.35	9.40	6.55
Kirkby	9.00	12.50	3.50	–	9.45	7.00
Up Trains	*am*	*am*	*pm*	*pm*	*am*	*pm*
Kirkby	-	11.35	4.20	6.30	9.30	6.45
Foxfield	9.00	11.45	4.30	6.40	9.40	6.50
Broughton	9.05	11.55	4.40	6.50	9.45	6.55
Woodland	9.20	12.10 *pm*	4.55	7.05	10.00	7.10
Torver	9.35	12.25	5.10	7.20	10.15	7.25
Coniston	9.50	12.40	5.25	7.35	10.30	7.40

In the winter months the schedule changed with only three trains leaving Coniston, the early afternoon train being omitted. On the 'Up' schedule, there was a (connecting) train from Kirkby at 7.10 am but no train at 4.20 pm. Other times varied slightly. Trains had either first, second and third classes or only first and second.

By the time the Coniston line was opened, copper was being increasingly resourced elsewhere as foreign supplies were tapped. Even so the mines would remain in business into the next century. Nevertheless, the carrying of passengers was soon seen as a vital role and as well as providing a service for the immediate locality, it was also realized that measures should be taken to enhance the tourist potential of the line. Tourism was taking hold and the market was expanding rapidly. The company, with this in mind, decided to take advantage of the proximity of Coniston Lake which could afford an obvious amenity. The Directors decided that in order to earn additional revenue, they needed to 'push the boat out'.

Foxfield Junction	7 20	12 45	..	..	6 35	..	..	8 55	..	..	6 50	..	..				
Broughton.............	7 30	12 50	..	..	6 45	..	..	9 0	..	..	6 55	..	..	8	8	6 4½	4½
Woodland	7 40	1 0	..	..	6 55	..	..	9 10	..	..	7 5	..	..				
Torver	7 50	1 10	..	..	7 5	..	..	9 20	..	..	7 15	..	..				
Coniston Lake ...	8 0	1 20	..	..	7 15	..	..	9 30	..	..	7 25	..	..	10	6	7 10	4 1½
Seascale (W'stwa'r)	8 33	1 53	..	..	7 38	..	..	10 3	..	..	7 58	..	..				
Whitehaven	9 15	2 35	..	..	8 15	..	..	10 45	..	..	8 40	..	..	16	0	12 2	6 3½
Workington	10 39	3 9	..	..	8 56	..	..	2 24	..	..	..	..	..				
Cockermouth.....	11 15	5 45	..	..	9 35	..	..	8 25	..	..	..	..	..				

▲ Stops by Signal if required.

BARROW AND CONISTON BRANCHES.

	WEEK DAYS.										SUNDAYS.			
UP.	1	2	3	4	5	6	7	8			1	2	3	4
	1 2 3	1 2 3	1 2 3	1 & 2	1 2 3	1 2 3	1 & 2	1 2 3			1 2 3	1 2 3	1 2 3	1 2 3
	Mxd	cl'ss.	cl'ss.	cl'ss.	cl'ss.	cl'ss.	cl'ss.	cl'ss.			cl'ss.	cl'ss.	cl'ss.	cl'ss.
	a. m.	a. m.	a. m.	p. m.	p. m.	p. m.	p. m.	p. m.			a. m.	a. m.	p. m.	p. m.
Fleetwood, *leave*														
Piel Pier about	Closed	during	the	Winter	Months.									
Barrow ....*leave*	5 50	9 0	12 0	1255	3 10	5 0	6 0	6 45			7 20	..	5 20	..
Furness Abbey	A	9 10	1220	1 0	3 20	5 10	6 15	7 0			7 30	9 15	5 30	7 15
Dalton	A	9 20	..	1 15	3 25	5 15	..	7 5			7 35	9 20	5 35	7 20
Lindal	A	9 25	..	..	3 30	5 20	..	7 10			7 40	9 25	5 40	7 25
Ulverston *arrive*	6 20	9 35	..	1 30	3 40	5 30	..	7 20			7 50	9 35	5 50	7 35
Kirkby	7 10	..	1235	..	..	..	6 30	..			8 45	..	6 40	..
Foxfield	7 20	..	1245	..	..	..	6 35	..			8 55	..	6 50	..
Broughton ..	7 30	..	1250	..	..	..	6 45	..			9 0	..	6 55	..
Woodland ..	7 40	..	1 0	..	..	..	6 55	..			9 10	..	7 5	..
Torver	7 50	..	1 10	..	..	..	7 5	..			9 20	..	7 15	..
Coniston l'k	8 0	..	1 20	..	..	..	7 15	..			9 30	..	7 25	..

BARROW AND CONISTON BRANCHES.

	WEEK DAYS.						SUNDAYS.			
DOWN.	1	2	3	4	5	6	1	2	3	4
	1, 2, 3	1, 2, 3	1 & 2	1 & 2	1 & 2	1, 2, 3	1, 2, 3	1, 2, 3	1, 2, 3	1, 2, 3
	class.	class.	class.	class.	class.	class.	class.	class.	class.	class.
	a. m.	a. m.	a. m.	p.m.	p. m.	p. m.	a. m.	a. m.	p. m.	p.m.
Coniston l'k	8 15	..	11 55	..	5 45	..	..	8 15	..	6 10
Torver	8 25	..	12 5	..	5 55	..	..	8 25	..	6 20
Woodland ..	8 35	..	12 20	..	6 10	..	..	8 35	..	6 30
Broughton ..	8 45	..	12 35	..	6 25	..	..	8 40	..	6 40
Foxfield	8 55	..	12 45	A	6 35	..	..	8 55	..	6 50
Kirkby	9 0	..	A	..	6 40	..	..	9 0	..	6 55
Ulverston *leave*	9 0	11 50	..	3.40	5 50	8 10	8 10	10 0	6 0	7 40
Lindal	9 10	12 0	..	3 50	..	8 20	8 20	10 10	6 10	7 50
Dalton	9 20	12 5	..	3 55	6 5	8 25	8 25	10 15	6 15	7 55
Furness Abbey	9 25	12 15	1 10	4 0	6 15	8 30	8 30	10 20	6 25	8 0
Barrow *arrive*	9 35	12 25	1 20	4 10	6 25	8 40	..	10 30	..	8 10
Piel Pier.........	Closed	during	the	Winter	Months.					
Dep. for F'wood										

▲ Stops by Signal if required.

ROOSE.—Nos. 2, 3, 5, and 6 Up, and 1, 4, and 6 Down Trains, on Week Days, and Sunday Trains, will stop when required.

ULVERSTONE MARKET DAYS. On Thursdays a Train will leave Carnforth for Ulverston at 7 46 after the arrival of Train from Kendal, Grange 8 40, and Cark 9 10 a.m.— Returning at 3 40 p.m.

THIRD CLASS Return Tickets will be issued from all Stations to Ulverston for No. 1 Up Train—Returning by 3 40 p.m. Down to Barrow—to Broughton and Coniston at 5 50 p.m.

The Furness and Ulverstone and Lancaster Railways, being only centre links in the chain of Through Communication, the Public is requested to take Notice that the Companies cannot undertake to guarantee that the Trains shall start from, or arrive at, any Station at the Time named in the Bill, nor will they be accountable for any loss or inconvenience which may arise from any delay or detention.

LUGGAGE.—The Companies will not be responsible for Luggage or Parcels left in any of their offices for the convenience of the owners ; but Passengers desiring such accommodation at Ulverstone or Furness Abbey may leave their Luggage on payment of a registry fee of 2d. each package.

TICKETS—First and Second Class Return Tickets are issued between all Stations at reduced fares ; those issued on Saturdays are available to return on Monday.

See General Notices and Regulations published at the Stations.

FLEETWOOD AND MORECAMBE STEAMERS : Discontinued during the Winter Months.

COACHES.

Cark Station, Cartmel, and Newby Bridge : Runs between Cark and Cartmel only.

Grange Station and Newby Bridge :

WILL LEAVE GRANGE on arrival of 11 16 a.m. Down Train, arriving at Newby Bridge at 12 40 p.m., and returns in time for the 4 19 p.m. Up, and 5 25 p.m. Down Trains. Ulverston Station and Newby Bridge : Discontinued during the Winter Months.

Coniston, Ambleside, and Hawkshead :

The "LADY OF THE LAKE" Coach leaves Coniston for Ambleside at 1 20 p.m.

From Ambleside to Coniston at 3 50 p.m.

OMNIBUSES from the Waterhead Hotel meet all Trains.

General Manager's Office, Barrow,   By Order,
November, 1859.   JAMES RAMSDEN, S. & G. M.

The timetable printed in *Soulsby's Ulverston Advertiser* on 17th November, 1859. It seems to indicate that initially there were through services to Kirkby.

The Steam Yacht Gondola

The first boat to be acquired by the company for use on Lake Coniston was named 'Gondola' (reflecting its outline and style). The vessel was assembled at Coniston Hall and launched on Wednesday 30th November. The *Lancaster Guardian* was once again there to record the event.

Launch of a Steamer on Coniston Lake

On Wednesday week the very interesting ceremony of launching the new steamer on Coniston Lake took place and was witnessed by a large concourse of spectators. The steamer, which is propelled by a screw is of a different construction and model of any hitherto introduced into the north and resembles most those known as the gondolas of Venice. In fact she is called a steam gondola and seems admirably adapted for rapid sailing and a light draught of water. The vessel is built of steel plates which were prepared and conveyed to the banks of the lake at Coniston Hall where the vessel was built and launched.

(There is a great deal of inconsistency encountered when referring to the SY *Gondola*. Some prefer to use just *Gondola* whilst others always refer to *The Gondola*. Certainly the latter is usually found in common parlance but also in some official communications.)

1860

Extension to the Copper Mines

In 1860 the extension to the Copper House (copper mines) was ready although there had been facilities for loading at the station before this link was made.

At the Directors' meeting on 16th February it was resolved to pay the Secretary £225. This would be paid for the period from the date the Act authorizing the building of the Railway had been passed, until 31st December and thereafter £50 per annum was reckoned to be the 'proper sum for the directors to pay', not, in fact, of the Coniston Railway but the Furness 'for his future services'. (Directors' Meetings were held on 8th August, 1860, 19th February, 1861, 7th August, 1861 and 28th February, 1862. The minutes get briefer and by this last meeting, some eight of the 132 pages in the impressive, beautifully bound dark green Minute Book had been used.)

The *Gondola* began regular service in June. The vessel attracted a great deal of attention and was featured in the *Illustrated London News* on 7th July when the following report appeared:

Steam Gondola on Coniston Lake

We this week present our readers with an Engraving of a most elegant and novel description of vessel built for the especial gratification of tourists to our beautiful English lakes. This vessel is in its outward form and internal fittings a perfected combination of the Venetian gondola and the English steam yacht - having the elegance, comfort and speed of the latter and the graceful lightness and quiet gliding motion of

On 7th July, 1860 *The Illustrated London News* saw fit to mark the introduction of *Gondola* with this illustration and a description of the vessel (*see text*). This is probably the earliest published image of the craft. Note the lack of a funnel. In the early version, *Gondola* was fitted with vents, presumably to avoid spoiling the clean lines of the boat's appearance. However, it seems there were problems with water entering these and so a conventional funnel was fitted.   *Author's Collection*

the former. It may be said to be the most elegant little steam-vessel yet designed and is specially suited for pleasure excursions on lake or river. *The Gondola*, as it is named, now floats on Coniston Water, Lancashire, one of the most charming of our lakes, recently made easily accessible to tourists from the metropolis and the chief towns by the extension of the Furness Railway to within a short distance of the head of the lake.

The vessel is of iron or rather steel plates. It is 85 feet long, beam 14 feet, draught of water only 4 feet 6 aft and one foot forward. It is propelled by a screw driven by a 16 horse-power engine on the locomotive plan, burning coke and placed quite aft, thus leaving the best part of the vessel for passengers and relieving them from smoke, smell and noise - three disagreeables generally complained of in ordinary steam vessels. The speed of the *Gondola* is from ten to twelve miles an hour.

The centre of the vessel being thus left free for passengers is fitted up as a saloon covered with a light roof; the sides of plate glass, in large sheets affording an uninterrupted view of the magnificent scenery surrounding the lake, the summit of the highest mountains being visible to those seated in the saloon.

The interior is beautifully finished in walnut wood and is cushioned and decorated after the style of the Royal carriages of our railways. The prow, which is long and graceful, is adorned with a well executed carving of the arms of the Duke of Devonshire, while the armorial bearings of the Duke of Buccleuch ornament the stern.

The vessel is the property of certain noblemen and gentlemen connected with the Furness Railway. It has been built to convey tourists round the lake at intervals during the day and for the use of private pleasure parties at other times.

The Gondola was designed by Mr James Ramsden, the secretary and general manager of the Furness Railway; it was built by Messrs Jones and Co. of Liverpool, under the inspection of Mr Douglas Hebson.

Very great credit is due to Mr Ramsden for the novelty of the design and for the tasteful manner in which all the details have been completed. The design has been patented.

The Gondola is commanded by one of those intrepid men who formed the crew of Sir Leopold McClintock in the recent voyage of the *Fox* to the Arctic regions.

The 'intrepid' man referred to at the end of the account was a certain Captain Anderson. He must have found Lake Coniston a marked contrast to the Arctic! He was followed by Mr Felix Hamill who was in charge of *Gondola* for some 50 years. In his later years Hamill had the real look of a seafaring man, not least because of his bushy beard. The engraving of *Gondola* in the *Illustrated London News* appears to show a vessel without a funnel. This is because, originally , the fumes from the coke fired burner were expelled through ducts which were almost horizontal, presumably to be inconspicuous and not detract from the clean lines of the design. However, there were problems with this design which, it seems, could let in water and a slender funnel, which was virtually upright, was later put in place.

1861

When the *Ulverston Advertiser* appeared on 19th December, the columns of print were edged with heavy black borders, the indication of a death of some significance. The Prince Consort had died. In this edition another death is reported, following an accident on the Coniston line. The account explains, in part, the reasons and also gives some insight into certain operational procedures.

On Saturday morning last, a serious and, we regret to say, fatal accident occurred at Foxfield Junction on the Whitehaven, Furness and Coniston railways. At this junction, the engines of the several companies exchange their trains of carriages which necessarily causes a great deal of shunting. We cannot fully describe the movements of the engines prior to the accident which we may here state took place on the departure of the first morning trains for Whitehaven, Ulverston and Coniston, so that it was dark. The Whitehaven train had left its train of carriages in their proper place and had shunted out of the way on the Coniston Branch. The Furness engine arrived and left its train in the proper place. The engine had then to take the Coniston train and it is usual to attach thereto in front of the engine a goods van for the Broughton Station which is only about a mile distant from Foxfield. It is the stoker's duty of the Furness engine to hook on this van and unhook it at Broughton, where it is pushed into a goods siding. The Coniston train being ready and the driver thinking the Whitehaven engine had backed clear of the line, started, the stoker remaining on the buffers of the engine ready to uncouple the van which he would have to do in a few minutes. Unfortunately, the Whitehaven engine was only shunting from off the Coniston line and the two engines, one going forward, the other backing, came into fearful collision, the van betwixt them killing instantly the stoker. The driver of the Whitehaven engine seeing that a collision was inevitable reversed the motive power and jumped off, as did his stoker, both being a good deal stunned by the leap. And here was another most alarming circumstance. The engine thus reversed started off up the Coniston line, passing Woodland where it came to a standstill for want of steam owing to the fire getting low and singular to say it did no damage to its runaway course. By a strange fatality the guard of the Furness train was father of the unfortunate stoker.

An inquest was held on the same day on the stoker, James Nelson Jnr, before William Butler Esq, coroner and a respectable jury of which The Revd Mr Robinson of Broughton was foreman. The jury viewed the scene of the accident and a verdict of 'Accidental Death' was returned. Mr Cook the active secretary of the Whitehaven railways and their officials were present.

1862

On the 16th May there was a Special General Meeting. The Duke of Devonshire, in the chair, proposed and Lord Cavendish seconded, a proposal which was resolved that the Bill to authorize the amalgamation of the Coniston Railway Company with the Furness Railway be approved. (As with the Directors' meetings, this final meeting resulted in only a very small fraction of the Minute Book being used.)

On 7th July the Act by which the Coniston Railway became part of the Furness Railway was placed on the Statute Book. So ended the independence of the Coniston Railway. In reality it had always only been an independent line on paper. Those who were on the Coniston Board were very much a part of the Furness Railway. The step was really inevitable.

Day to Day Running, the First 10 Years

The fact that the Furness Railway had taken over the Coniston Railway at Board level made little difference to the normal operating routines, the Furness having been in at this level from the outset. An insight into the day to day operation of a small railway such as the Coniston Railway can often be found by reading the messages sent from 'on high' with instructions or comments about procedures. A number of these instruction sheets sent to various station masters at Coniston are still extant. Mr Cloudsdale was the first recipient at Coniston.

One area, which often gave rise to problems on the smaller lines in this period, was the use of the telegraph. There are many situations when the telegraph is either being used in the wrong way or too 'enthusiastically'. It may well have been that the comparative novelty of this system resulted in over zealous use. The Coniston line was no exception, it seems. On 11th December, 1860 it was pointed out that several telegraph messages between Barrow and Coniston were being 'interrupted'.

'Serious consequences could result . Any of the company's servants found doing this will be dismissed immediately'. Again, on 23rd February, 1863, a general order went out:

Great inconvenience has been caused from telegraph clerks and station masters fighting for possession of the wires when they were required for most important purposes. You will please note that when the prefix GM is given, you at once give way. This prefix takes precedence of all other messages, commercial or railway and will only be used by the General Manager or by his special order. When the message sent under the above prefix is finished, the party last in possession of the wires must have next preference. All messages to be as concise as possible.

On a different subject, on 7th March, 1861 it was decreed that:

Ordinary 1st and 2nd Class tickets must be issued by express train to all L&NW stations. Passengers wishing to be booked to Manchester L&Y must be booked to Preston and for Leeds Midland to Lancaster only.

There was an arrangement whereby company employees who were injured at work would be attended by a doctor. So, on 7th January, 1863:

Herewith I hand you a book for the purpose of requesting the attendance of the surgeon to any of the company's servants. The report must be sent to the Secretary of the Provident Society at Barrow and you should see that it is returned in due course properly signed by the surgeon.

On 18th December, 1861 there was a missive about bobbin wood:

The above [bobbin wood] sent from your station will in future be carried at machine weight only, ordinary special class rates must be charged less 20%. The charge for loading will, of course, be made as usual [from James Ramsden].

There were numerous missives sent about rates and revision of rates. In January 1860 John Barrett of Coniston Mines was issued with new tariffs and a copy of these was sent to the Coniston station master. In the same month costs for the carriage of livestock also went up. There was also the directive that in future no less a quantity would be charged for than half-a-waggon load 'Nor will a larger number be allowed for half-a-waggon load than 3 head of cattle, 12 sheep, 12 calves or 12 pigs. [However] If carried in the guards van, to and from local stations, sheep 6d. each, calves and pigs 9d. each'.

The charge for horses and carriages was also specified. Horse and Carriage (2 wheel 41s.; 4 wheel 43s.). Railway amalgamations and the resulting arrangements for goods also gave rise to a considerable number of instructions. A notice from the London & North Western Railway was passed on to Coniston. It concerned the transporting of gunpowder, much of which would be used in the mines. The information is so important that the label 'to Coniston' is written in red. The directives are that there must be no more than four and a half tons per van; the vans must be locked; vans must not be loaded on Saturday or (must be loaded) early enough on Friday that arrival early on Saturday is possible because gunpowder must not remain in the stations during Sunday. (William Caukwell is the originator of this.)

There had clearly been some queries because gunpowder was transported in barrels and so this directive was up-dated with the instruction that there must not be more than 100 barrels per waggon and that each barrel must not contain more than 100 lb. of gunpowder. Even dogs and pianos were taken account of in the way of things. On 7th June, 1865 Mr Cloudsdale was informed that dogs could be carried between 1 and 10 miles between local stations for 3*d*. per dog. A piano (upright or grand is not specified!) 'is to be charged as a four wheeled carriage when conveyed by passenger train on carriage trucks in road vans belonging to the sender or double parcel rates when not'.

On 26th July, 1862 there were instructions relating to the installation of a new weighing machine. 'All copper, slate and other heavy goods must be put over your machine and charged for accordingly. Also test the coal waggons occasionally to prove the correctness of your invoices'. Some instructions resulted from complaints. One of these related to the station clocks and the fact that there were inaccuracies noted. On the 13th October, 1863 an edict went out reminding the station master at Coniston that clerks in charge of attending to the station clock should note carefully the telegraphed time and sent on a daily basis 'fingers should be moved to the correct time as soon as the message is received'. On the 28th September, 1863 new 10 ton ore waggons were introduced. These were only for use by the Earl of Balcarras. They would be sent up to Coniston with coal. There would be one day for discharging them or two shillings a day would be levied thereafter. In October, Kirklees Hall was allowed to load the company's waggons with coal. Waggon hire was charged at the rate of 8*d*. per ton.

Early in 1866 the railway braced itself to deal with the outbreak of what was then referred to as Cattle Plague; presumably what in modern parlance has become Foot and Mouth Disease. Initially a licence from the magistrates was needed if animals were to be received but very soon it was resolved that 'no bull, cow, heifer or calf should be accepted on any station on this line' [that is, the Furness Railway]. Notices continued to appear throughout 1866 and there was a particular emphasis on the cleansing of waggons and that thereafter they should be well whitewashed with lime. In September of 1867 a note saying cleansing was no longer necessary has 'Cancelled' written across it in brown crayon and the message about cleansing was still being reinforced in October of that year. However, on 2nd November, the restrictions were relaxed but it was not until 1st June, 1870 that all orders relating to 'Cattle Plague' were formally cancelled.

On 19th June, 1867 Mr Cloudsdale received a rather unusual sort of directive. It concerned the SY *Gondola*. The distance between the station and the pier from which *Gondola* sailed was quite considerable and not a little difficult to negotiate and it appears there had been complaints from some passengers that by the time they reached the pier, the *Gondola* had left. Hence the directive.

In future the *Gondola* must not sail from the Pier before 12.30 in order to allow passengers time to get down from the train. [A contingency plan was then outlined should the train be delayed.] A flag staff will be fixed at the station and when the train is more than half an hour late, the flag will be hoisted for the *Gondola* to leave.

The elevated position of the station presumably made this signal easy to see!

By 1st August Mr Gracie had taken over from Mr Cloudsdale.

There seems to have been something of an issue about coach proprietors coming on to Coniston station to meet passengers and disagreements in the process. (Similar occurrences had happened elsewhere on other railways.) Mr Gracie received the following communication:

Mr Ramsden has give permission to Mr Dove to come onto the platform in the same way as Mr Atkinson has been allowed to get passengers and their luggage for the coaches - in fact all coach proprietors are to have the same privilege - but if they misconduct themselves by quarrelling or annoy the passengers in any way you must send them out and not let them onto the Company's premises. H. Cook. Barrow. [Mr Atkinson had been afforded a further privilege, from 15th June, 1861, when it was agreed that he could receive a copy of *The Times* newspaper sent free from Carnforth to Coniston, at the Waterhead Hotel.]

In 1871 it was noted that staff were having difficulties checking large numbers of paper tickets involved with 'pleasure parties'. To avoid this it was decided that a card ticket would be issued in future to each passenger and 'one of the party, as well as having a ticket will have a ticket with advice to show [collectors] for what station the tickets are issued'.

The instruction issued on 11th February, 1871 might well raise a few eyebrows in this day and age:

Company's Workmen and Telegraph Line Men in their working clothes are in all cases to travel Third Class (when there is a Third Class carriage on the Train). But if there are no Third Class carriages on the Train by which they have to travel they may also go to a Second Class compartment - one without cushions - and when practicable they must all go in a compartment by themselves.

Furness Railway 2-2-2 well tank No. 37 had a driving wheel of 5 ft 6 in. in diameter. This locomotive was built by Sharp, Stewart in 1866 and is known to have worked on the Coniston branch. It was withdrawn in 1898. Originally the engine offered rather less protection to the crew, being fitted with just a weatherboard.   *R.W. Rush Collection*

1872

In 1872 there was 'An Act Authorizing the Furness Railway to Provide and Use Steam and Other Vessels on Windermere and Coniston' (35 & 36 Vict.). This act, in effect, simply formalized what had been happening on Coniston for 12 years and recognized that it was, in actuality, the FR which was operating the service even though *Gondola* was registered in Ramsden's name.

The Concluding part of the 19th century and the beginning of the 20th

1893

In the 1893 timetable the pattern remained very much the same with usually four up trains and four down trains. (In this and all subsequent timetables described, 'down' trains run *to* Coniston.) There was an additional up train on Thursdays. The timings had been altered and these were now as shown.

	Weekdays		Th			Sundays	
	am	am	am	pm	pm	am	pm
Coniston	7.20	9.10	10.45	2.35	4.40	8.05	6.40
Torver	7.26	9.16	10.51	2.41	4.46	8.11	6.46
Woodland	7.35	9.25	11.00	2.50	4.55	8.20	6.55
Broughton	7.43	9.33	11.08	2.58	5.03	8.28	7.03
Foxfield	7.47	9.37	11.12	3.02	5.07	8.32	7.07
Foxfield	8.23		11.23	3.08	5.18	8.53	7.18
Broughton	8.27		11.27	3.12	5.22	8.57	7.22
Woodland	8.34		11.34	3.19	5.29	9.04	7.29
Torver	8.43		11.43	3.28	5.38	9.13	7.38
Coniston	8.50		11.50	3.35	5.45	9.20	7.45

Th = Thursday only service.

In addition to the services shown, there was also a train leaving Broughton at 8.13 am and arriving at Foxfield at 8.17 am. This provided a connection with the 8.22 am to Barrow Central.

1897

In May the Coniston branch was fitted with Tyer's Electric Tablet system and this replaced the staff and ticket method of working the line. This system remained in use until 1958 and the end of passenger services.

There was an even greater drive during this period to make the use of the Coniston branch more attractive to those visiting the Lake District. One aspect involved improvements and enlargements to the stations and a series of plans were drawn up to this effect. The plan for Broughton is dated 26th April, that for Woodland 23rd April, for Torver, 27th April and for Coniston, 7th May.

1898

In a report written on 16th July by Colonel Yorke it was noted that at Broughton a new signal box had been built at the side of the level crossing with its gates being worked from the box. It was protected by signals and the box had nine levers in use with five spare. It was also observed that the line was worked on the electric tablet system and Broughton was a tablet station and was used for allowing passenger trains travelling in opposite directions to pass. However, this was done by one of the trains being shunted into the yard through the siding points and the report comments that such a procedure was contrary to the Board of Trade requirements and therefore 'I cannot recommend the Board to sanction the use of this place for this purpose in its present condition'. The report goes on, 'A second platform should be built and a proper passing loop constructed and until this is done, passenger trains should not be permitted to pass each other here'. As far as Woodland was concerned, the report notes that:

… a new passing loop has been laid in here, an up platform constructed and a new signal box and signals provided. The down platform has a waiting room, ladies room and conveniences for both sexes and the up platform has a waiting shed. The signal box contains seventeen working levers and the interlocking is correct.

There is, however, a requirement relating to the gradient at that section:

Owing to the gradient, runaway catch points should be laid in at the lower end of the down platform. As this will necessitate shortening the platform at this end it will be necessary to lengthen the platform in front of the signal box at the Torver end of the loop and probably to shift the points leading into the siding further towards the north.

The report deals next with Torver:

There is a ground frame here containing two levers to work a siding connection at the south end of the station. The line is single, worked in the electric tablet system and the station has only one platform. Torver is not a passing place nor tablet station and as the ground frame is correctly locked by the electric tablet no signals are fixed or required.

There are no requirements listed at Torver. At Coniston it is noted that 'additional platform accommodation has been provided, a new line has been laid in, additional connections and sidings constructed, a new signal box built and the whole place signalled. There are now three platforms all signalled for the arrival and departure of trains. The signal box contains thirty-three working levers, two spaces and one spare lever and there is also a ground frame at the north end of the station containing fifteen working levers which are bolt locked from the main signal box'. The requirement is that Nos. 33, 34 and 21 in the signal box should lock No. 35 release lever in both positions.

The Board considered the report and pointed out that they were ready to authorize the construction of a second platform at Broughton. However, the Directors did point out that it would not be convenient to place the new platform opposite the existing one because of the differing levels and the goods sidings.

X. Torver - There is a ground frame here containing two levers, to work a siding connection at the South end of the station - The line is single, worked on the electric tablet system, & the station has only one platform. ~~Torver~~ Torver is not a passing place, nor tablet station, & as the ~~points~~ ground frame is correctly locked by the electric tablet fixed on no signals are required -

Requirements. nil -

XI. Coniston. Additional platform accommodation has been provided here, a new loop line has been laid in, additional connections & sidings constructed, a new signal box built & the whole place resignalled -

There are now three platforms, all signalled for the arrival & departure of trains.

The signal box contains 33 working levers, 2 spaces, and 1 spare lever, & there is also a ground frame at the north end of the station containing 15 working levers, which are both locked from the main signal box.

Requirements. Nos. 33, 34 & 21, in the signal box to lock No 35 release lever in both positions -

Part of the report written by Colonel Yorke on 16th July, 1898. This section refers to Torver and Coniston.

Whitsuntide excursions seem to have been particularly popular and the following year (1899) The Albert Memorial Schools from Queen's Road in Manchester organized an outing on Whit Thursday which took in Coniston and a chance to take a sail on *Gondola* (return fares 1s. 6d. and 1s.).

1900

In 1900, one of the railway's most notable users (perhaps *the* most notable) John Ruskin, the internationally famous writer and art critic, died. He had moved to Brantwood, which overlooks Coniston, in 1871, turning a run-down property into a splendid house. His travels all over Europe would usually begin and finish on the line. On arriving back from Seascale in June 1889, from what turned out to be his last journey on the railway, Ruskin spoke to Edward Woolgar, the station master. Woolgar comments:

> On [Ruskin] arrving back here, when I opened the carriage door, he said 'I've returned earlier than anticipated but I wanted to be a home again. There's no place like Coniston'. He leaned on my shoulder on getting out of the train and I assisted him into his own carriage. When passing through the waiting room he said 'Now don't you go away and leave us. We have got to know and like you. I don't want to see a strange face when I next come'. On reaching his carriage he shook hands with me and as I helped him in he repeated, as with an effort 'There's no place like Coniston - no place like Coniston'. His head sank wearily forward as the carriage drove off.

Woolgar visited Ruskin in April 1899 and this was to prove his last visit before Ruskin died in January the following year.

Edward Woolgar was not born in the locality but in Yarmouth on the Isle of Wight on 27th May, 1860. When his father retired as a master mariner he brought his family to Newby Bridge and took charge of the Furness boats on Lake Windermere. Son Edward was on the railways all his working life. Eventually he became station master at Coniston in 1888. In 1902 he moved to Grange-over-Sands, then to Ulverston, retiring in 1920. He died in February 1950 and during much of his retirement, whilst living back in Coniston, was involved to a great extent in public service. This included being a magistrate and curator of Coniston Museum and he became a county alderman in 1944. By all accounts, Edward Woolgar was delighted to have associations with Brantwood. After he moved on from Coniston to Grange and Ulverston he was often called upon to do favours for the Severns (part of the Brantwood 'set') which included finding lost items on trains and arranging (road) carriages. On his last visit to see Ruskin, Woolgar, a man of literary and artistic taste, was made a presentation by him although Woolgar does not record of what this consisted.

This station staff photograph at Ulverston *circa* 1917 shows Edward Woolgar seated third from left.

The Furness Railway steam railmotor and trailer car, which was designed by W.F. Pettigrew, at Coniston.   *J.M. Bentley Collection*

1903

The various works at the stations had been completed and on 3rd June the Board sought permission to start using the second platform at Broughton. On 8th June the Directors were informed by the Board of Trade that Major Druitt would come 'as soon as possible'. By 23rd October the various matters had been resolved and a copy of a letter from Major Druitt was sent out by Herbert Jekyll stating that the Board of Trade had sanctioned the new works at Broughton station. In his report Major Druitt noted that the new platform was 350 ft-long and that it had not been possible to place the new platform opposite the original one. He commented:

> … in order to enable trains to pass each other when standing at either platform it is necessary for the up train to use the usual down loop line and vice-versa as the platform on the proper up side is at the down end of the platform on the proper down side. [He then added (possibly fearing that these observations might suggest there were irregularities)] I see no objection to this unusual arrangement.

The points and signals at the up end were worked from the ground, bolt locked from the signal box which had 14 working levers and one spare lever with the ground frame having 11 working levers and one spare lever, all of which were in order.

1905

An innovation during the summer of this year was the introduction of the railmotor and trailer (referred to further under 'Motive Power'). This rather unusual form of motive power had originally been used on the Lakeside branch but had not gone down too well in some quarters and there had been complaints about the quality of the ride. A new refreshment room at Coniston was ready and opened during July but it was reported, at the time, that 'There are not, as yet, many resident visitors to the village notwithstanding the favourable weather lately prevailing'. There was a large influx of visitors over the weekend of 24th-25th June when special trains were chartered by the Catholics living in Barrow. On Saturday some 3,000 went to Coniston on two trains and on Sunday, as well as a trip to Workington, there was another train to Coniston, this time carrying some 700 people. It seems the days were spent 'boating on and driving round the lake' together with 'rambles on the fells and to the waterfalls in the vicinity of the village'.

1908

The success of *Gondola*, which was reflected in the marked increase, towards the end of the century, in the numbers who had taken a trip on the vessel, prompted the FR under Alfred Aslett's guidance, to commission another boat which would be capable of carrying twice as many people (400 compared to the 200 of *Gondola*). In 1908, a new vessel, *The Lady of the Lake*, was launched at Waterhead. This larger

Furness Railway poster announcing the arrival of the new vessel *Lady of the Lake*.

vessel had a bow section which had an appearance not unlike the front of a kayak used by North American Indians. She was built by Thorneycroft of Southampton, had twin cabins, a speed a of over 10 knots and was some 90 ft long. The Furness Railway, keen to promote this development, issued a special poster in connection with this service. The poster had in bold print 'Coniston. New Steam Yacht - *Lady of the Lake'*. On the left of the picture and standing high on the hillside, an elegant lady is daintily waving her handkerchief at the new vessel standing at the jetty far below. There is a highly romanticized view across Coniston which is bathed in a golden glow. The poster advertises Tourist, Weekend and Day Excursion tickets for June, July, August and September and the use of the steamers in connection with Circular Tours Nos. 2 and 4 and also with coaches from Ambleside to Coniston and Greenodd to Lake Bank.

There is some evidence that Felix Hamill took command of this new vessel and the charge of commanding *Gondola* passed to a Captain Priss. However, whilst Captain Priss certainly did do duties on *Gondola*, Captain Hamill remained, effectively, master of *Gondola*. (He clearly had a great affection for the vessel; he even built a model of it!) The Furness Railway had planned to take *Gondola* out of service once *The Lady of the Lake* was fully operational (what would have happened to Felix Hamill?) but *Lady of the Lake* never achieved the popularity of *Gondola* and it seems public opinion backed the retention of *Gondola* which was kept in service as a result. The tours referred to in the poster were introduced to try and promote tourism further into the district. These were to a large extent on the initiative of Alfred Aslett (who had succeeded Ramsden). One tour for example, started, in effect, at Fleetwood and took in a sea trip, railway journey, a journey in a horse-drawn carriage and, of course, a trip on Lake Coniston; all for just over 10s. first class.

There are tickets for the essential 'circular' part of some of these tours extant. For tour No. 1, the left-hand side of a third class ticket, which in one direction was for the section of the journey from Lake Side to Coniston via Broughton and Ambleside to Lakeside by steamer, is coloured bright pink. The right-hand section of the ticket, which was for the coach journey from Coniston to Ambleside, is a buff colour. The travellers went from Lake Side via Broughton to Coniston and then on to Ambleside by coach. On arriving at Ambleside, they took the steamer down Windermere and so back to Lake Side. For this tour taken in the opposite direction, the left-hand side of the ticket was for the sections from Lakeside to Ambleside, by steamer, and then from Coniston to Lakeside via Broughton. The right-hand section of the ticket was for the trip from Ambleside to Coniston. The left-hand side of a first class ticket was coloured yellow and right-hand buff, as before.It might be concluded from this that pink was the distinguishing colour for third class tickets and yellow for first class. Presumably as the coach section was the same for first and second classes the colour could be the same. A first class ticket for tour No. 2 was buff with a horizonatal yellow band across the middle and a thin diagonal yellow band from top left to bottom right on the left-hand section. The left-hand section of the ticket was for the trip from Lake Bank to Coniston, by *Gondola*, and thence by rail to Greenodd via Ulverston by rail. The right-hand section of the ticket was for the journey from Greenodd to Lake Bank by coach. Tour No. 4 also included sailing on *Gondola*.

Gondola at Water Head pier, Coniston, with passengers disembarking from *Lady of the Lake* in the background.

Author's Collection

Lady of the Lake arrives at Lake Bank pier, Coniston.

A postcard view of *Gondola*. In the distance is the Waterhead Hotel. The card is postmarked 1904.   *Author's Collection*

This postcard depicts *Gondola* and the boat house, Coniston.   *Author's Collection*

Gondola and Boat House, Coniston

Both *Gondola* and *The Lady of the Lake* were popular subjects for picture postcards and these were produced in considerable quantities at various times and throughout almost the whole of the period when the vessels were operating. Raphael Tuck probably went further than others and actually produced a set of cards called the 'Furness Railway Steamer Series' which proved to be very popular (and are still very collectable). Other publishers included F. Frith, Hartmanns, Peacock Brand and G.P. Abraham Ltd (of Keswick).

1912

The period just before World War I saw something of a heyday for the passenger services. In the summer of 1912 the timetable was as follows:

Weekdays	am	am	am	am	am	pm	pm	pm	pm	pm	pm SO
Coniston	7.30		8.40	11.05	11.50	2.25	4.15	6.00	6.25		8.45
Torver	7.37		8.46	11.11	12.08	2.39	4.33	–	6.31		8.51
Woodland	7.48		8.54	11.19	12.08	2.39	4.33	–	6.39		8.59
Broughton	7.56	8.41	9.02	11.27	12.16	2.47	4.41	6.17	6.47	7.52	9.07
Foxfield	8.00	8.45	9.05	11.30	12.20	2.50	4.45	6.20	6.50	7.55	9.10

Weekdays					pm						
Foxfield	8.14	8.55	9.20	11.55	1.40	3.20	5.10	6.25	7.10	8.15	9.20
Broughton	8.18	9.00	9.23	11.59	1.45	3.23	5.13	6.30	7.13	8.18	9.23
Woodland		9.08		12.07	1.53	3.30	5.20	6.38		8.25	9.30
Torver		9.19		12.14	2.04	3.37	5.28	6.49		8.32	9.38
Coniston		9.25		12.20	2.10	3.45	5.35	6.55		8.40	9.45

SO = Saturdays only.

There was also a Sunday service.

	am	pm	pm	pm
Coniston	9.00		6.35	8.00
Torver	9.06		6.41	8.06
Woodland	9.14		6.49	8.14
Broughton	9.22		6.57	8.22
Foxfield	9.25		7.00	8.25
Foxfield	10.00	2.57	7.25	
Broughton	10.03	3.00	7.28	
Woodland	10.10	3.07	7.35	
Torver	10.18	3.18	7.43	
Coniston	10.25	3.25	7.50	

Perhaps with all these extra visitors anticipated thought was given to the greater comfort of female passengers. A ladies' lavatory was made at Torver station. This involved taking some space from the waiting room and the porters' room. The work was completed on 14th March, 1912.

World War I

In 1914 the country was precipitated into the first of two major world wars. In the Directors' report for 1914, it is pointed out that:

> ... in pursuance of an Order in Council made on 4th August, 1914 under the provisions of the Regulation of the Forces Act 1871 the control of the Furness Railway and docks was taken over by the Government for which purpose the Railway Executive Committee was appointed composed of general managers of certain companies with the President of the Board of Trade as Chairman ...

The two steam vessels were laid up. It was assumed all pleasure excursions would cease; not an altogether accurate forecast.

In spite of ongoing hostilities in a war which was to drag on longer than early, over optimistic, predictions suggested, it seemed to have very little impact on the Coniston branch. Figures show that in 1913 the copper exports of the UK amounted to 3,006,800 tons. A comparison was made with the figure of 2,663,600 tons for Germany, although with the Austrian figure of 476,700 tons these two were the greater by 130,000 tons. Some 317,800 tons of Germany's copper goods came to the UK with only 18,300 tons going the other way. This, it was suggested, made Germany the loser as far as copper goods were concerned. These figures had little impact at Coniston. The copper mines were no longer in the forefront of production. However, in what might have been an unexpected development it was reported that over the weekend of 31st July-2nd August, 1915, Coniston and district 'experienced its busiest holiday weekend in its history'. Visitors came 'long distances' and had booked apartments whilst a brief holiday granted at Vickers' works resulted in many coming for respite. Monday was particularly busy with people arriving for the day 'by train, car and cycle'. This was repeated to some extent when the Furness Railway advertised a cheap day excursion from Barrow to Coniston on 29th August. The train left Barrow at 2.15 pm. The return fare was 1s. 6d. It was announced about this time that from 1st September, the 1.40 pm from Foxfield would depart in future 40 minutes later. It is reported that 'there was also a slight curtailing of the steamer services on the lake', so it would seem the boats were brought out again.

On Monday 7th September, 1915 a poignant event took place in Coniston. At 8.00 am a procession set off from the Church Bridge. At the head of this procession was a band and this was followed by 11 men who had volunteered for active service in the war. They arrived at the station in time to catch the 8.40 am *en route* for 'Ulverstone' where there were to join the main body of the 4th Battalion of the Kings Own. They were given a rousing send off complete with fog detonators and to the strains of the National Anthem as the train left. The line was also able to help in the war effort when, in September, the Furness Railway sought accommodation in Coniston for munitions workers and there was a good response. At the time there was already a large number of men from Coniston working in Barrow and it was decided that the numbers which would be travelling would justify a special train for workmen.

During the war the passenger services were fewer, although not significantly so and trains were still run on Sundays.

The summer timetable in 1916 was as follows:

Weekdays								SO	Sundays	
	am	am	am	pm	pm	pm	pm	am	pm
Coniston	7.25		10.55		2.45	4.30	5.45	9.15	6.35
Torver	7.31		11.01		2.51	4.36	5.51	9.21	6.41
Woodland	7.39		11.09		2.59	4.44	5.59	9.29	6.49
Broughton	7.47	8.41	11.17	1.05	3.07	4.52	6.07	9.37	6.57
Foxfield	7.50	8.44	11.20	1.08	3.10	4.55	6.10	9.40	7.00
Foxfield	8.10	8.55	11.45	12.57	3.20	5.15	6.15	10.00	7.20
Broughton	8.13	8.58	11.48	1.00	3.23	5.18	6.18	10.03	7.23
Woodland		9.06	11.56		3.31	5.27	6.27	10.11	7.31
Torver		9.14	12.04		3.39	5.34	6.34	10.19	7.39
Coniston		9.20	12.10		3.45	5.40	6.40	10.25	7.45

SO = Saturdays only.

The Period following the War

The period following the end of World War I was a difficult one for the railway companies. The Government had taken over the railway system and the companies had anticipated that once the war was over, the lines would be returned to them and, presumably, things would go on very much as before. This, however, did not happen. The Government seemed reluctant to hand back the control of the lines to the various Boards of Directors and, in effect, therefore, the shareholders. Alarm was voiced in many railway boardrooms about this and motives were questioned about why this was happening. The cost of running the railways certainly had increased considerably during the war and there were those who felt that by retaining control, the Government was hoping to get back some of the costs.

Whilst that may have been true, at least in part, it eventually became apparent that other factors were being considered which would have a far reaching effect on the operation of Britain's railway system. The plan was to merge all the various small companies into just four large ones, the London Midland & Scottish Railway, the London & North Eastern Railway, the Southern Railway and the Great Western Railway.

In spite of what some perceived as gathering storm clouds on the (national) railway scene, there was a resumption of normality. The steamers started to ply the lake again and the country in general anticipated a return to better times. These, sadly, were to be short-lived.

At the end of this significant era, with the 'Grouping' of all railways into four main companies about to take place, passenger services returned to a pattern similar to that before the war.

Furness Railway 0-6-0 No. 118 with a goods train at Coniston *circa* 1910. *J.M. Bentley Collection*

The railmotor for a Coniston branch train stands at the platform in this busy scene at Foxfield. Note the ultramarine and white livery of the coaches nearest the camera.   *F. Moore*

Summer services

Weekdays	am	am	am	am	pm	pm	pm	pm	pm	pm
Coniston	7.15		9.10	10.35	1.20	2.40	4.30	5.50	6.30	7.45
Torver	7.21		9.16	10.41	1.26	2.46	4.36	5.56	6.36	7.51
Woodland	7.29		9.24	10.49	1.34	2.54	4.44	6.04	6.44	7.59
Broughton	7.37	8.25	9.32	10.57	1.42	3.02	4.52	6.12	6.52	8.07
Foxfield	7.40	8.30	9.35	11.00	1.45	3.05	4.55	6.15	6.55	8.10
Foxfield		8.40		11.55	2.10	3.30	5.17	6.35	7.05	
Broughton		8.44		11.58	2.14	3.33	5.21	6.39	7.08	
Woodland		8.51		12.06	2.21	3.41	5.28	6.46	7.16	
Torver		8.59		12.14	2.29	3.49	5.36	6.54	7.24	
Coniston		9.05		12.20	2.35	3.55	5.42	7.00	7.30	

Compared with the timetable for 1912, there was an extra service on Sundays, making four in each direction

Sundays	am	am	pm	pm	pm
Coniston	8.55	11.00		6.25	8.00
Torver	9.01	11.06		6.31	8.06
Woodland	9.09	11.14		6.39	8.14
Broughton	9.17	11.22		6.47	8.22
Foxfield	9.20	11.25		6.50	8.25
Foxfield	10.05	11.45	2.57	7.15	
Broughton	10.08	11.48	3.00	7.18	
Woodland	10.16	11.46	3.08	7.26	
Torver	10.24	12.04	3.16	7.34	
Coniston	10.30	12.10	3.20	7.40	

When the Grouping of the railways was implemented, the Coniston Line, as part of the Furness Railway, passed into the control of the London Midland & Scottish Railway (LMS).

Motive Power in the Period up to the Grouping

The last of the Bury 0-4-0 locomotives, with bar frames, was built for the FR in 1861 by W. Fairburn & Sons. However, this type of locomotive had a tender and given the proviso that tank engines must be used on the line when it first opened, these 0-4-0s would have been precluded from service. It is probable, therefore, that it was 2-2-2 well tanks, built by Sharp, Stewart, which operated in the early days.* The early versions did not have a cab roof. The driving wheels had a diameter of 5 ft 6 in.; the carrying wheels, 3 ft 6 in. The water was carried in a tank which was situated below the bunker and between the frames. Later versions of these locomotives had a basic cab which was little more than a weatherboard turned at the top to provide a roof and extended at the rear to the bunker. In 1873 the Sharp, Stewart 2-4-0s (which had a tender) were introduced and may well have seen service on the line. However, by 1896 some of these locomotives had been rebuilt as 2-4-2 tank engines which made them

---

* Ahrons comments that 'after 1858 the single driver tank engine almost died out. A few were built as late as 1866 by Sharp, Stewart & Co. for the Furness Railway'.

much more suited to branch line service and at least two of them survived to see post-Grouping operations.

In 1914 a new type of locomotive was introduced for the purpose of working, amongst other lines, the Coniston branch. This locomotive was designed by W.F. Pettigrew, who had taken over as locomotive superintendent of the FR after Mason retired in 1896. The new tank engine, which had a 4-4-2 wheel arrangement, had particularly fine proportions and was very elegant. The design reflected, in some degree, Pettigrew's previous experience on the London & South Western and Great Eastern railways. These locomotives were built by Kitson & Co. and the Vulcan Foundry and had driving wheels of 5 ft 8 in. They were still active at the Grouping and beyond.

Probably the most notable motive power used on the branch in this period was the railmotor. This was also designed by Pettigrew. It was built at Barrow and first appeared on the line in 1905 after being transferrred from the Lake Side branch. There was a steam engine at one end of the main coach body and also a trailer coach. There were12 first class seats and 36 third class seats. The trailer car could accommodate 34 third class passengers. In spite of complaints about its poor riding qualities, the unit had the distinct advantage, as far as the line was concerned, of having the facility to be driven from either end, so obivating any need for reversals. It ran until World War I.

Initially coaches of the four-wheeled variety were used on the line but these were soon replaced by six-wheelers. These coaches, used during the Furness period, carried Furness livery of the deep blue ultramarine and white. This livery was also carried by the railmotor.

One of the elegant W.F. Pettigrew Furness Railway 4-4-2Ts of 1914. This portrait of No. 11084 (formerly FR No. 42) at Coniston shows the locomotive resplendent in LMS livery.
William Nash Collection

Chapter Four

Post-Grouping and Nationalisation, LMS and British Railways, 1923-1962

Like many similar branch lines, the effect of the Grouping had little immediate impact on the Coniston branch. There would be some changes in motive power but routines would remain largely unchanged and for the next 16 years the line simply went on serving the communities through which it passed. It seems that in the main, visitors, especially those who came for the day, preferred to go to Windermere and Ambleside or Keswick and so there were surprisingly few specials. The geography of the location of the line was probably, also, a contributory factor to this state of affairs. However, the London Midland & Scottish Railway continued to operate the two steamers and the tours were also still operated. In 1936, the company produced a special six page leaflet in an attempt to promote visits to Coniston and trips on the steamers. The leaflet is rather low-key, in promotional terms, although in order to try and give more appeal to the outings, a number of photographs are included in addition to the timetables it contains.

The Introduction of Camping Coaches

An innovation in the 1930s was the introduction of so-called camping coaches. This mode of accommodating holiday-makers had proved popular elsewhere. Three such coaches were put in at Coniston and one at Torver. They remained in use until World War II and then, with the cessation of hostilities, the ones at Coniston were brought back into use but not the one at Torver. It would seem that by the 1950s they were not in great demand and by the end of that decade all of them had gone.

World War II

The year in which World War II began heralded some changes although not so much in the day-by-day running of the line because it had no real strategic importance. However, there were changes on the tourist front as the curtain came down for many on the facilities to take an annual holiday. One result was that the second vessel introduced by the FR to Lake Coniston, *The Lady of the Lake*, was taken out of service. *Gondola*, after many years of service to the tourists visiting Lake Coniston, had already been laid up in 1936 for what may have seemed the final time. There was to be some ignominy but eventually a happy outcome in the saga of this vessel.

The timetable, as set out in the 'LMS Emergency Passenger Services', issued in September 1939 reads as follows:

A classic postcard view of *Lady of the Lake* on Coniston. This card was postmarked 1930.

Author's Collection

Postcards were produced showing various scenes of the railway and the steamers. This one, in the Frith's Series, was published by T. Satterthwaite, Central Café, Coniston and numbered 82796. It shows *Gondola* and *Lady of the Lake* moored alongside the jetty at Lake Head and was produced in the 1930s. This particular card was sent in 1936 by Mr and Mrs Robinson to Edith, and the writer observes 'I think this is the nicest place we have seen in this part up to now...'

Author's Collection

Ex-FR Pettigrew 4-4-2 No. 11084 is seen arriving at Coniston with a train of six-wheelers in the 1920s. This scene is captured by the camera of young Cumbrian William Nash, taken whilst he was still a teenager. The book *Cumbrian Railway Photographer* (Oakwood Press, 2002) presents many of Nash's railway photographs from around the region. *William Nash Collection*

Ex-Furness Railway Pettigrew 0-6-0 No. 12501 (ex-FR No. 20) at Coniston on 6th June, 1935.
H.C. Casserley Collection

Ex-Lancashire & Yorkshire Railway Aspinall 2-4-2 Radial tank No. 10644 on the branch train near Coniston, 6th June, 1935.   *H.C. Casserley*

LMS Fowler '3F' 0-6-0T 'Jinty' No. 16406 stands next to the water column at Coniston, while the train crew are in deep conversation, 6th June, 1935.   *H.C. Casserley*

A busy scene at Coniston in 1937 with an LMS Fowler '3F' 0-6-0T 'Jinty' awaiting departure.
Author's Collection

A close-up of the 'Jinty' waiting to depart. Notice the Furness Railway ground signal in the foreground.   *R.M. Casserley Collection*

Foxfield and Coniston (One class only)

Down	am	am	S pm	pm	pm	pm
Foxfield	6.39	8.53	1.02	5.06	6.05	7.10
Broughton-in-Furness	6.41	8.55	1.04	5.08	6.07	7.12
Woodland	6.48	9.02	1.11	5.15	6.14	7.19
Torver	6.56	9.10	1.19	5.23	6.22	7.27
Coniston	7.03	9.17	1.26	5.30	6.29	7.34

Up				S		
Coniston	6.00	7.18	12.23	4.25	5.33	6.34
Torver	6.05	7.23	12.28	4.30		6.39
Woodland	6.12	7.30	12.35	4.37		6.46
Broughton-in-Furness	6.18	7.36	12.41	4.43	5.49	6.52
Foxfield	6.22	7.40	12.45	4.47	5.53	6.56

The 'S' denotes 'Saturday Only' and it is seen that the 5.33 pm from Coniston was not scheduled to stop at either Torver or Woodland. There was no Sunday service. This timetable was not particularly austere given the prevailing circumstances.

In 1940, *Supplement No. 2 to the General Appendix to the Working Timetables* issued in December, contains a terse note concerning speed restrictions. 'Between Coniston and Foxfield - up and down trains - 40 miles per hour.'

When hostilities became intense and the threat to life very real, many schools in the London area and in the south, generally, decided the wisest move would be to relocate. A considerable number moved to the South-West. One exception was Roedean, the girls' school, which took up residence in the Keswick Hotel and also used parts of the railway station as classrooms. Bembridge School, in the Isle of Wight, also relocated to the Lakes. This move came about partly because the founder of Bembridge, John Whitehouse, was a great devotee of John Ruskin and so the obvious choice of a place to relocate for the period of the war was Coniston. Whitehouse owned Brantwood and was minded to use it for the school. However, he was persuaded that for a number of reasons it would be unsuitable and so he purchased the Waterhead Hotel, which happened to be up for sale, and Bembridge relocated there. At the beginning of term, Bembridge travelled from Euston with Mill Hill School, which had relocated at Saint Bees. Some pupils from Sedbergh, Rossall, Stoneyhurst and Giggleswick schools, returning north for the start of term, also travelled on this train. The coaches carrying Bembridge and Mill Hill took a route which avoided Barrow *en route* to Foxfield. The Bembridge pupils left the train at Foxfield but as there were less than 90 of them, it would seem no special train was needed and they travelled to Coniston on a scheduled service. On the return trip the Bembridge pupils left Coniston at 6.55 am.

1946

World War II had been over for a year and a period of readjustment began. Things, generally, would never be quite the same again and this was true for the nation's railways as in many other aspects of life.

With the useful life of *The Lady of the Lake* being considered past, the vessel was broken up for scrap. It seems that the ignominy for *Gondola*, referred to earlier, also began when the engine was removed and apparently used to power a sawmill in Ulverston. A little later, the hull became a houseboat. To step beyond the lifetime of the railway for a moment and move to the year 1963, a storm rendered the hull of *Gondola* unusable. Shortly afterwards, she was deliberately partly submerged in a specially made channel near the shore of the lake in an effort to preserve what remained of the vessel. The hulk was left there until raised in 1975 when the National Trust 'refurbished' *Gondola* which was recommissioned in 1980. She can now be seen once again on Lake Coniston and visitors are able to enjoy the experience of sailing in this splendid craft. The 'refurbishment' was, of necessity, extensive, and little of the original remains! Even so the boat provides an evocative taste of what life was like in what many wish to think of as more halcyon days.

1948

By 1948 the post-war changes mentioned earlier involved a major change for Britain's railway system when they were nationalised on 1st January, 1948. Once again, however, this seemed to have little impact on lines such as the Coniston branch, which continued with 'business as usual'. The timetable issued by British Railways in September 1948 shows, in many ways and perhaps not surprisingly, a very similar pattern to what had gone before, although there were more trains:

Foxfield and Coniston (Third class only)

Weekdays only					E	S					
	am	am	am	am	pm	pm	pm	pm	pm	pm	pm
Foxfield	6.39	7.55	8.46	10.22	12.35	1.03	4.00	5.08	6.12	7.15	8.52
Broughton	6.41	7.58	8.48	10.24	12.37	1.05	4.02	5.11	6.14	7.17	8.54
Woodland	6.48		8.55	10.31	12.44	1.12	4.09		6.21	7.24	9.01
Torver	6.56		9.03	10.39	12.52	1.20	4.17		6.29	7.32	9.09
Coniston	7.03		9.10	10.46	12.59	1.27	4.24		6.36	7.39	9.16

	am	am	am	am	am	pm	pm	pm	pm	pm	pm
Coniston	6.00	7.22		9.20	11.55	3.25	4.27		6.39		8.22
Torver	6.05	7.27		9.25	12.00	3.30	4.32		6.44		8.27
Woodland	6.12	7.34		9.32	12.07	3.37	4.39		6.51		
Broughton	6.18	7.40	8.12	9.38	12.12	3.43	4.45	5.52	6.57		8.40
Foxfield	6.22	7.44	8.15	9.42	12.17	3.47	4.49	5.55	7.01		8.44

'E' signifies 'Except Saturdays' and 'S' signifies 'Saturdays Only'.

It can be seen that services along the branch are now supplemented by the ones operating between Foxfield and Broughton only. The 8.22 pm from Coniston does not stop at Woodland. In spite of the war being over, there are still no trains on Sundays. Even so, the service on weekdays is a generous one.

Coniston signal box, 14th May, 1950.   *H.C. Casserley*

A view from the northern end of the platform of the train shed at Coniston.

R.M. Casserley Collection

1950

As the war years and the austerities that people had had to endure receded further, the 'annual holiday' began to be a feature of people's lives again. However, it was not considered viable to reintroduce steamer services to Lake Coniston. In any case the *Lady of the Lake* had been dismantled.

Further, even though tourism was once again beginning to make an impact on the region there were significant changes emerging in the pattern and these would have a profound effect on the railway. The first was the growing number of bus tour operators and the flexibility of this mode of transport. This, however, was only the first wave of what might be seen as an onslaught on the viability of the railways. The second and, potentially, more damaging was the greater and more widespread use of private motor cars. The railway network at large, but especially rural branch lines, would be subject to considerable financial pressures. Operating deficits would become commonplace. The Coniston branch was no exception; in fact it was to become one of the early casualties, certainly as far as the North-West was concerned.

Even so, during this period, it continued to serve the local community and was treated with a sort of affection common to many small branch lines serving rural communities. The crews were local men and had a rapport with the travelling public, many of whom were known to them. The service they often gave, though unofficial, would extend beyond what might be described as the call of duty. There was the antiques dealer who lived at Bowmanstead, just to the south of Coniston. On his return trips from London the crew would make an unscheduled stop at Bowmanstead to allow him to get off and so avoid the long walk home from Coniston. There is the story of the small boy who used to holiday with his parents at Coniston and who in the late 1950s would be taken for footplate rides from Coniston to Foxfield and back. He had something of a shock when, on one occasion, he was allowed to sit in the driver's seat and the fireman was the only other person present. Suddenly, much to his consternation, the train lurched into action without, it seemed, anybody driving. It was only later that the mysteries of the push-pull system were explained and that the driver was in the 'coach' at the other end of the train! These days would not last very much longer.

After nationalisation, British Railways (Midland Region) made some attempts at continuing to promote Coniston in its strategy for tourism. Holiday Runabout tickets were issued. In 1956, for example, these were available between 29th April and 26th October. Area No. 2 was the Lancashire Coast and the Lake District, and Coniston was included in the destinations. The tickets, for third class travel, cost 21s. and could be used for six days; Sunday to Friday inclusive. Dog tickets could be purchased for 5s. 3d. and cycle tickets for 10s. 6d. There was a service from Blackpool to Coniston on Tuesdays and Thursdays. The departure time from Blackpool Central was 8.45 am with arrival at Coniston at 12.23 pm. On the return the train left Coniston at 5.47 pm and arrived at Blackpool Central at 9.10 pm. There were various pick up points *en route*.

These two rare views taken at Foxfield depict ex-LMS AEC diesel multiple unit Nos. 79740-2 while on a short-lived trial on the Coniston branch in 1954. The trial was not a success; the diesel unit was unable to cope with the gradients on the branch.   *(Both) A.J. Postlethwaite*

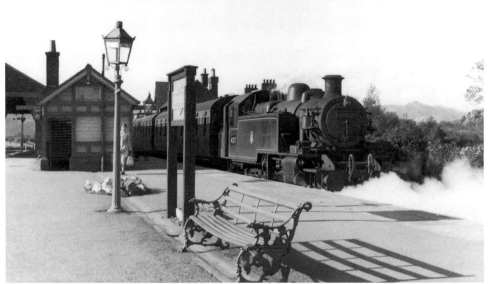

Ex-LMS Ivatt class '2' 2-6-2T No. 41217 on the Coniston branch service at Foxfield on 4th September, 1952.   *T.J. Edgington*

Sister engine, No. 41221, is the branch engine in this view taken at Foxfield.   *N.K. Harrop*

HOLIDAY RUN-ABOUT TICKETS

AREA No. 2.

LANCASHIRE COAST

AND

LAKE DISTRICT

29th APRIL to 26th OCTOBER 1956

Third **21/-** Class

CHILDREN UNDER 14 HALF FARE

Tickets are not transferable and must be signed by the holder.

DOG TICKETS 5/3   CYCLE TICKETS 10/6

issued in conjunction with the above.

AVAILABLE FOR SIX DAYS SUNDAY TO FRIDAY INCLUSIVE	UNLIMITED TRAVEL ON ANY TRAIN BETWEEN ANY STATIONS WITHIN THE AREA

No allowance or extension of date can be granted on these tickets in consequence of there being no Sunday Service in certain areas.

Travel in Rail Comfort

BRITISH RAILWAYS

Cover of Holiday Runabout Tickets pamphlet, 1956.

SPECIAL
THROUGH TRAIN SERVICES
TO AND FROM
THE LAKE DISTRICT

MONDAYS TO FRIDAYS ONLY
18th JUNE to 14th SEPTEMBER 1956

OUTWARD	MW FO	T.Th O	C SX	RETURN	MW FO	T.Th O	C SX
	am	am	am		pm	pm	pm
Blackpool Central ...dep.	8 45	8 45	9 50	Windermere.........dep.	...	...	6 45
Blackpool South .... ,,	8 49	8 49	9 54	Kendal .... ,,	...	...	7 9
Squires Gate............. ,,	8 54	8 54	9 59	Oxenholme .... ,,	...	...	7 21
St. Annes .... ,,	8 59	8 59	10 4	Coniston .... ,,	...	5 47	...
Ansdell .... ,,	9 4	9 4	10 9	Broughton .... ,,	...	6 3	...
Lytham .... ,,	9 9	9 9	10 14	Foxfield .... ,,	...	6 8	...
Kirkham .... ,,	9 20	9 20	...	Lake Side............... ,,	6 3	...	...
Southport Chapel St. ,,	9a25	9a25	10a 0	Ulverston .... ,,	6 34	6 44	...
Preston .... ,,	9 58	9 58	10 52	Grange.................... ,,	6 52	6 59	...
Lancaster ....arr.	10 24	10 24	11 16	Arnside .... ,,	7 2	7 6	...
Hest Bank .... ,,	...	...	11 24	Silverdale .... ,,	7 10	7 12	...
Carnforth .... ,,	10 36	10 36	11 31	Carnforth .... ,,	7 23	7 23	7 38
Silverdale .... ,,	10 46	10 46	...	Hest Bank .... ,,	7x 1	7x 1	7 43
Arnside .... ,,	10 52	10 52	...	Lancaster .... ,,	7 35	7 35	7 54
Grange .... ,,	11 0	11 0	...	Preston ....arr.	8 3	8 3	8 23
Ulverston .... ,,	11 15	11 15	...	Southport Chapel St. ,,	8z54	8z54	10z10
Lake Side .... ,,	11 50	...	...	Kirkham .... ,,	8 29	8 29	8 56
Foxfield .... ,,	...	11 52	...	Lytham .... ,,	8 44	8 44	9 6
Broughton............... ,,	...	11 56	...	Ansdell .... ,,	8 49	8 49	9 10
		pm		St. Annes............... ,,	8 55	8 55	9 15
Coniston .... ,,	...	12 23	...	Squires Gate .... ,,	9 0	9 0	9 20
Oxenholme .... ,,	...	...	11 57	Blackpool South...... ,,	9 5	9 5	9 25
			pm	Blackpool Central... ,,	9 10	9 10	9 30
Kendal .... ,,	...	...	12 5				
Windermere............ ,,	...	...	12 25				

a—Runs 25th June to 7th September Inclusive, Change at Preston.   z—Change at Preston.
c—Runs 18th June to 7th September Inclusive. MWFO—Mondays, Wednesdays and Fridays Only.   T.Th.O.—Tuesdays and Thursdays Only.   SX—Saturdays Excepted.   x—Change at Lancaster.

SOUTHPORT - BLACKPOOL
MONDAYS to FRIDAYS 25th JUNE to 7th SEPTEMBER 1956

	am			pm
Southport Chapel Street ....dep.	10 0	Blackpool Central.........................dep.	6 2
St. Luke's .... ,,	10 2	Blackpool South............................ ,,	6 7
Hesketh Park .... ,,	10 5	Preston ....arr.	6 30
Churchtown .... ,,	10 7	Churchtown .... ,,	7 7
Preston .... ,,	10 35	Hesketh Park .... ,,	7 9
Blackpool South ....arr.	10 55	St. Luke's .... ,,	7 13
Blackpool Central .... ,,	11 0	Southport Chapel Street .... ,,	7 17

FOR FULL DETAILS OF TRAIN SERVICES SEE PASSENGER TIMETABLES OR ENQUIRE AT STATIONS OR AGENCIES

Extract from Holiday Runabout Tickets pamphlet, 1956.

No. 41221 veers off onto the Coniston branch at Foxfield.   *N.K. Harrop*

The junction at the north end of Foxfield station on 27th December, 1957. Rebuilt 'Royal Scot' class 4-6-0 No. 46151 *The Royal Horse Guardsman* heads a southbound express. The Coniston branch curves away to the right.   *P.B. Booth/N. Stead Collection*

Ivatt class '2' No. 41217 awaits departure from Coniston on 4th September, 1952.

T.J. Edgington

This close-up of the same train sees the locomotive beneath the lattice footbridge. This structure was later bought by Patrick Satow and moved to the Ravenglass & Eskdale Railway where it was sited at Ravenglass station until January 2004 (*see photograph page 92*). *T.J. Edgington*

The first of two views taken of the northern portal of the train shed at Coniston. Ivatt class '2' No. 41221 bears the legend 'BRITISH RAILWAYS' on its side tanks, while the notice boards visible in the background read 'LONDON MIDLAND AND SCOTTISH' in this view taken on 14th September, 1950. *H.C. Casserley*

Little has changed six years later. No. 41217 is the train engine on 27th December, 1957. Just visible on the extreme right of the picture the notice boards now read 'BRITISH RAILWAYS'. *P.B. Booth/N. Stead Collection*

1957

It seems to be during the early part of 1957 that rumours began to circulate suggesting closure of the line might be in the air. In spite of this, in April, there was something of a boost for the railways and certainly for those in the North-West when petrol rationing gave a fillip to the number of people travelling on the trains.

At the same time the Ribble Bus Company put forward proposals that included lowering the fares for short journeys. In April, with Easter and days-out in the offing, the trips by train advertised included the Coniston branch with the price of a ticket from Barrow being 3s. 3d. There were also Football Excursions to Barrow on Good Friday, Saturday and Easter Monday and these included Coniston and stations on the line. Even so, there was a poignant indicator of the way things were moving when, later, it was reported that the level of road traffic had broken all previous records. In May, the Ribble Bus Company was denied permission to lower some fares but the company still held out the hope that cheaper fares would come eventually. In this they were unduly optimistic.

Another possibly significant move for the railways of the area was made in May when the British Transport Commission announced a proposal to include Barrow as a regional HQ. The area, it was anticipated, would take in Lancaster, in the South, to Keswick, in the North. It was stressed these were still only proposals. In fact it was some time before they materialized. In July the competition from Ribble seemed to lessen when it was announced fares would be increased. Although there was no bus service from Broughton to Coniston at this stage, this was seen, overall, as a step which might give the railways an advantage, albeit slight.

It was in August that the first real indication of what was in the minds of those responsible for managing the railway system in this area became clearer. The *Barrow News* carried an item of news headed 'Railway To Coniston May Be Closed Down'. It was suggested this might well happen before the end of the year. The reason given was quite simply that the line was not economical. British Railways would make no comment at this stage about the possible date of closure but it was alleged that a decision had already been made. This was because it was known that the Divisional Education Authority at Ulverston had addressed the issue of problems in transporting children to a new secondary school in Coniston when the closure became effective. The road up to Coniston was described as 'bad' and it was argued that it was unlikely that economic road transport would be possible. The North West Transport Users Consultative Committee would have to be involved in a final decision but already it was being argued that even in summer the line had failed to pay its way. (As if by some portent, the film *Gone with the Wind* was then showing at the local cinema at the time.)

This was the first significant closure of its kind to be mooted in this area and the mechanism for protest was not readily in place as it would be for similar situations in the years ahead. Battle lines were soon drawn up as various bodies and individuals prepared to demand the retention of the line. On Thursday, 12th September, there was a meeting of the Barrow Trade Council. The members voiced 'strong protests' at the proposed closure of the line. The meeting was

Looking south from the platform at Coniston on 27th December, 1957 towards the signal box and engine shed.   *P.B. Booth/N. Stead Collection*

A splendid view of Coniston station on 27th December, 1957 which shows off nicely the elegant footbridge. Passenger stock can be seen at the northern end of the train shed and an Ivatt class '2' awaits departure with a short goods train.   *P.B. Booth/N. Stead Collection*

informed that BR was arguing the case on the estimated saving of £17,000 if the branch was closed. However, those present felt that if the rail connection was lost, people would find it difficult to get to Barrow and this would have an adverse effect on trade. The suggestion was made that economies could be effected by reducing the number of coaches used on the trains.

Mr Montgomery pointed out that 'the Lake District is difficult enough of access' and therefore taking this step (of closing the line) would be a serious one to take. A further suggestion was that the introduction of diesel trains to replace the steam trains might help.

On Tuesday, 24th September, there was a meeting of the Transport Users' Consultative Committee (TUCC) in Manchester where it was announced that a local enquiry would be held. A number of objections had been made by various groups and individuals. Sir Patrick Hamilton, the Chairman of the TUCC, said the meeting would take place in November. He also noted that closing the line would save £16,679 plus maintenance and the renewal of station buildings.

There was also the matter of improving the road to Coniston should closure take place and consultation with the County Council would be necessary about this. Perhaps determined to be undeterred by what was happening, in October, Coniston station under station master Mr J.R. Lawrence took fourth place and gained a third class award in the 'Best Station Garden Competition' for the region. Further, the station was given a second class award for tidiness and cleanliness.

During the same month it was announced that the Lake District Planning Board had 'joined the fight' to save the line. At a meeting on Tuesday, 1st October it was agreed that the General Purposes Committee should be summoned to a 'special' meeting if it seemed advisable to make representation at the meeting to be held in November. Mr Hawkins felt 'We ought to oppose the closure of this line as strongly as possible'. A number of parish and rural councils had also expressed concerns about the proposal, it seemed.

Later in the month the higher fares which the Ribble Bus Company had been seeking were sanctioned. It was announced that Friday, 8th November would be the date for the meeting with the TUCC and the venue would be Coniston Institute. At this stage Lancashire County Council agreed to join the protest against closure.

So it was that against the background, on the one hand, of mounting concern about the H-Bomb (the latest nuclear weapon) and much local press coverage speculating what might be the outcome if such a device was dropped on Barrow and, on the other hand, the celebrations after Donald Campbell once again succeeded in breaking the water speed record with an overall speed of 239 mph on Lake Coniston, a small group gathered at 11.00 am on the morning of 8th November at the Institute in Coniston to fight for the future of the line which had served them for almost a century.

'Had BR forgotten that it was in control by virtue of the fact the railways had been taken over by the State for the benefit of the People?' was how one speaker saw the crux of the matter. Sir Patrick Hamilton was in the Chair. The argument for closure was essentially an economic one. The line was losing money and there seemed little hope of reversing this. A count had shown that there were

A quiet moment at Coniston on 8th August, 1958. Note the more modern ground signal in use by this stage (*see page 63*).   *R.M. Casserley*

Foxfield station looking north on 2nd August, 1958. There appears to be a considerable activity around the Coniston branch train.   *R.M. Casserley*

about 226 passengers on the weekdays in the winter and 218 in the summer. Saturday figures gave 194 in the winter and 322 in the summer. These figures excluded the 'Specials' which could number three each week with some 1,000 visitors. The meeting was informed that closure was unlikely to occur before the following Easter and after that there would still be a freight and parcels service.

The body of objectors had agreed to have one spokesman, Mr F.D. Youle, the Clerk to Ulverston Rural District Council. He represented Lancashire County Council, the Lake District Planning Board, the Friends of the Lake District, Barrow and District Chamber of Trade & Commerce and Lancashire Education Authority. He put forward a number of objections including the fact that one hundred school children would be affected after 1959 when the new secondary school would be opened at Coniston. The matter of using diesel trains was raised again and the meeting was told that these had already been tried on the line but it had been decided the use of such trains would not make substantial savings. The outlook for retaining the line was looking bleak.

On Saturday, 7th December, Sir Ian Fraser MP spoke on the matter when opening a Christmas Fair at Coniston. The Minister of Transport had informed Sir Ian, in a reply to a question regarding the Coniston branch, that no Public Enquiries would be held before local lines were closed down. However, Sir Ian told the assembled company that he intended to raise the matter in the House of Commons. He then went on to make a long speech supporting the retention of the line. The issue rumbled on to the end of the year and, again, the problems of road transport were aired.

1958

On Tuesday 10th June, 1958, the North Western Area TUCC held a meeting and agreed to support the closing of the line to passengers. The main reason given, not surprisingly, was that the line was losing at least £16,000 per annum. Apparently the decision seemed to come as a surprise in some quarters because a sub-committee had previously recommended that the line should be retained.

There was a proviso to this decision, namely whether or not a suitable bus service could be run to replace the rail service. This had been discussed earlier and it had been pointed out road transport to Coniston was seen as a problem because the road was in such a poor state. Although the Traffic Commissioners had already said they would approve a bus service from Foxfield to Coniston there was also the matter of a road restriction order proposed by Lancashire County Council. This body had said that the cost of making the Broughton to Torver route fit for heavy buses would 'be considerable' and it had planned to seek a restriction order which, if approved, would involve banning vehicles of more that 50 cwt and so could restrict the route to small coaches.

At the same time, Ribble Motors had expressed a willingness to operate the route and had made application to do so. In connection with this, a long public meeting had taken place at Ulverston involving the Traffic Commissioners. A few weeks later, towards the end of August it was announced that Ministry approval had been given for Ribble to run a bus service between Broughton and Torver if (an important 'if') British Railways decided to close the Coniston branch. The service would actually operate between Foxfield and Coniston. Strangely, in the same week, British Railways stated that no definite decision had been made about the future of the line. (It was, in fact, still only a proposal!) Then the Minister of Transport confirmed the Lancashire County Council application for a restriction order prohibiting heavy vehicles from using the road between Broughton and Torver. This confirmation was subsequently modified to allow the use of 'stage carriages'; in other words the Ribble buses! Nevertheless, it was made clear that no other buses, be they excursion services, express services or private party coaches, would be allowed to use this stretch of road. Still, at this juncture, there was the qualification 'if the Coniston line is closed'.

With a certain inevitability that was to be become all too apparent with the later proposals to close other lines, in September the decision had been made. The Minister of Transport had decided the branch should be closed and this step was supported by the TUCC when it met on Tuesday, 16th September. It was pointed out that although the line would remain open for freight, it would not be used for excursion traffic. In reply to a question as to whether the line might be used if the road became blocked by snow or impassable for whatever reason, it was said trains 'might be run'.

On 26th September, a letter appeared in the *Westmorland Gazette* inviting people to come forward if they would like to travel on the 'last train' on Saturday, 4th October. The line would be closed officially as from Monday 6th October. This letter was in some ways very pertinent. During the meeting of the TUCC, Sir Patrick Hamilton had been asked whether 'anything special' had been arranged for the last passenger train trip or if there was to be any celebration of the centenary of the line. Sir Patrick is reported as replying, 'The less of that the better. Rather we should have a celebration of the new bus service'. It would clearly have to be enthusiasts who would mark the event! And mark it they did.

The last passenger train was officially the 8.52 pm from Foxfield to Coniston (although it did have to work back 'empty' to Barrow and some, it seems, stayed on for this trip). The locomotive was '2P' class 2-6-2T No. 41217. The driver was Mr J.A. Watson, of Coniston, and the fireman was Mr R. Gaitskill. The guard was Mr A. Wallace. A board was placed on the front of the engine and on this was the inscription 'Foxfield-Coniston. 41217. Oct 4/58 The End'. The last ticket sold was No. 6921 and the final passenger to get on the train was Mr J. Mansergh, a student, who left it until the last moment to do so. There were about 100 people who travelled (some 40 enthusiasts and the rest were local people, apart from a small group representing BR). Rain fell as the train left for Coniston.

Detonators had been placed on the line and somewhere in one of the compartments a group of girls sang a current hit song *Last Train to San Fernando*. There was much conversation and, for the older passengers, a lot of reminiscing about the days when the service had been something of a lifeline and about characters such as Willie Reddan, George Hodgson and Mr Stackhouse, all once associated with the branch. And then it was over. Five minutes late into Coniston - but five minutes extra at the end of an era. The train then returned 'empty' to Barrow and passenger services were no more.

'Ribble' Takes Over

From 6th October, 1958 the Ribble bus company introduced its 'New Service' between Coniston and Foxfield. The first run on weekdays left Coniston at 5.51 am and arrived in Foxfield at 6.25 am. There were four buses each weekday with one additional service between Broughton and Foxfield. The last run of the day from Coniston left at 4.30 pm. Buses from Foxfield started at 6.35 am and the last of the four runs up to Coniston left at 5.58 pm (although it appears this was soon changed to 6.08 pm). There was an additional service between Foxfield and Broughton. On Sundays, there was an 11.09 am and an 8.05 pm from Coniston and a 1.00 pm and 8.50 pm from Foxfield. An additional service ran each way between Broughton and Foxfield. In spite of the comments allegedly made by Sir Patrick Hamilton, nobody seems to have seen fit to organize a celebration for the introduction of this new bus service! Linked in with the new service was the revision of the one which operated between Coniston and Ambleside.

During the period when discussion about closure had been rife, the electricity company, NORWEB, made a very astute move. In the early 1960s a new transformer was needed for the sub-station near the railway station at Coniston. Getting such a piece of equipment to Coniston by rail was comparatively easy but would have been extremely difficult by road. Some far sighted individual, working for NORWEB, made the decision to have a transformer installed that had something of the order of 10 times the capacity needed for Coniston at that time but would be adequate for a considerable period after closure of the line. The outcome was that this piece of equipment duly arrived at Coniston by rail!

It is also reported that, later, after the line closed, a crew was sent to Coniston to collect the branch engine, which was shedded there. This locomotive, together with items of stock, was to be taken back to Barrow. The engine, which usually faced 'up-hill' towards Coniston had only ever been connected at the bunker end to the front of the two coaches (and ran push-pull fitted). This meant that the couplings and pipes at the smokebox end were never used. This resulted in a big problem for the crew when they coupled up the rolling stock to the front of the locomotive. The rubber brake pipe, which had not been moved off its mounting for a very considerable period, split and, as a result, during the journey down the line, it was not possible to maintain the brake vacuum needed to keep the brakes off. The members of the crew struggled to rectify the situation using rags and whatever they could find to check the leaking vacuum pipe. They were very late reaching Foxfield and worked the engine so hard to get back to Barrow in reasonable time that the locomotive firebox firebars, together with the fire itself, fell down into the ashpan!

1961

What might well be seen as the last significant working on the branch took place on 27th August when an enthusiasts' special from Manchester ran on the line as part of a tour of Furness rails. Motive power on that occasion was class '4F' 0-6-0 No. 44347.

R I B B L E

NEW SERVICE

501   CONISTON – BROUGHTON – FOXFIELD

from 6th October, 1958 until 13th June, 1959

DOES NOT OPERATE ON SUNDAYS

						S		S				S	
Coniston, Crown Hotel ....dep.	5 51	7 12	....	....	11 9	....	....	3 15	....	4 30	8 5	....
Torver, Church House Inn .... ,,	6 0	7 21	....	....	1118	....	....	3 24	....	4 39	8 14	....
Jct. Road to Woodland Station..... ,,	6 12	7 33	....	....	1130	....	....	3 36	....	4 51	8 26	....
Broughton, Square................. ,,	6 21	7 42	....	8 15	1139	....	1219	3 45	....	5 0	8 35	....
Foxfield, Railway Station .... arr.	6 25	7 46	....	8 19	1143	....	1223	3 49	....	5 4	8 39	....

						S		S				S	
Foxfield, Railway Station ....dep.	6 35	7 54	....	8 41	1155	....	1 0	3 55	....	8 56	8 50	....
Broughton, Square................. ,,	6 39	7 58	....	8 45	1159	....	1 4	3 59	....	6 0	8 54	....
Jct. Road to Woodland Station:..... ,,	6 48	....	....	8 54	....	....	1 13	4 8	....	6 9	9 3	....
Torver, Church House Inn .... ,,	7 0	....	....	9 6	....	....	1 25	4 20	....	6 21	9 15	....
Coniston, Crown Hotel............ arr.	7 9	....	....	9 15	....	....	1 34	4 29	....	6 30	9 24	....

S Sats. only.

608   6.42

REVISED WINTER SERVICE

669   AMBLESIDE – CONISTON

from 6th October, 1958 until 15th May, 1959

	NSu	NSu	NSu	S	NSu		NSu	NSu	NSu	S		S
Ambleside, Ribble Bus Station ......dep.	5 22	7 17	9 11	1040	1234	1 34	2 46	4 34	6 4	7 36	8 0	9 20
Skelwith Bridge Hotel .... ,,	5 32	7 27	9 21	1050	1244	1 44	2 56	4 44	6 14	7 46	8 10	9 30
Glen Mary, Saw Mill .... ,,	5 43	7 38	9 32	11 1	1255	1 55	3 7	4 55	6 25	7 57	8 21	9 41
Coniston, Crown Hotel............. ,,	5 51	7 46	9 40	11 9	1 3	2 3	3 15	5 3	6 33	8 5	8 29	9 49
Coniston, Boon Crag Wall Post Box.. arr.	....	7 50	9 44	....	1 7	2 7	....	5 7	6 37	....	8 33	....

	NSu	NSu	NSu	NSu		NSu	NSu	NSu		S	S
Coniston, Boon Crag Wall Post Box..dep.	7 51	....	9 45	1 10	....	2 10	5 10	....	6 40	8 35	
Coniston, Crown Hotel............. ,,	7 55	9 15	9 49	1 14	1 34	2 14	5 14	6 30	6 44	8 39	9 24 9 50
Glen Mary, Saw Mill .... ,,	8 3	9 23	9 57	1 22	1 42	2 22	5 22	6 38	6 52	8 47	9 32 9 58
Skelwith Bridge Hotel .... ,,	8 14	9 34	10 8	1 33	1 53	2 33	5 33	6 49	7 3	8 58	9 43 10 9
Ambleside, Ribble Bus Station ...... arr.	8 24	9 44	1018	1 43	2 3	2 43	5 43	6 59	7 13	9 8	9 53 1019

S Sats. only.   NSu Not Suns.   *6.45   7.14*

— SEE OVERLEAF FOR FARES TABLES —

Tickets are issued and passengers are carried subject to the General Regulations and Conditions of the Company contained in its official Time Tables available on request.

RIBBLE MOTOR SERVICES LTD.   Phone

Head Office   ..   **FRENCHWOOD, PRESTON**   4272
Local Offices   ..   **AMBLESIDE**   ..   ..   Market Cross   3233
    ULVERSTON   ..   ..   The Ellers   3196

mb 3m (rep.) 3/11/58

The Ribble timetable showing the bus service introduced between Coniston and Foxfield immediately after the line closed. Note the amended times marked on in ink.

Left: Foxfield signal box which controlled the junction for the Coniston branch.

Lens of Sutton Collection

Below: 'Jinty' 0-6-0 No. 47564 leaves Coniston with a goods train on 3rd August, 1958. *A. Moyes*

The first of a series of four photographs that track 'Jinty' 0-6-0T No. 47317 and the branch goods on 1st June, 1960. The first view is taken at Broughton-in-Furness station.   *John Spencer Gilks*

'Jinty' 0-6-0T No. 47317 on the level crossing at the south end of Woodland station on 1st June, 1960.   *John Spencer Gilks*

No. 47317 on the branch goods train at Woodland station on 1st June, 1960.   *John Spencer Gilks*

'Jinty' 0-6-0T No. 47317 on the branch goods train at Torver station on 1st June, 1960.
John Spencer Gilks

1962

Freight services did continue but these only lasted a further four years. The *Barrow News* of Friday 27th April carries a news item headed 'No More Trains After Monday' (30th April) and the article points out that the line to Coniston would close completely and all goods would, in future, have to be taken by road. It seems there had not really been a great demand for freight services and so throughout the time the line was fully open, there had been only one freight working each day. After passenger services ceased, the freight working was reduced to three days each week or 'on demand'.

The *Evening Mail* of 27th April contains a photograph which it claims is of the last freight to arrive in Coniston. The locomotive, a '3F' class 0-6-0 tank engine, appears to be working bunker first. Reference is made in the caption to the enthusiasts' special which was run the previous year.

Removal of the track started in 1962. At this stage all the stations were intact but during the following years Coniston was allowed to deteriorate until in 1968, in spite of hopes that some use might be found for it, it was demolished.

Motive Power after the Grouping

After the Grouping of 1923, locomotives of companies other than the former Furness Railway started to appear on the branch and over the years down to and beyond nationalisation. Lancashire & Yorkshire tank engines designed by Aspinall took over from the Furness 4-4-2s. The fact that the rail motor could be driven from both ends made for greater ease of operation and when these tank engines appeared they were used in conjunction with a push-pull system, removing the need for the engine to run round the train. These locomotives were followed, in turn, by London & North Western tanks. These were Webb's 2-4-2s. It is reported that this class did not prove powerful enough to operate successfully and struggled to get up Broughton bank, barely able to haul two fully-loaded carriages. The outcome was that they were replaced and the Lancashire & Yorkshire tanks reinstated. During the late 1930s, Fowler 2-6-2T locomotives were in evidence on the line from time to time, working in connection with excursion trains from Blackpool.

At the end, Ivatt 2-6-2T locomotives were operating the push-pull services, usually either No. 41217 or 41221. These were in charge of two coaches. The allocated locomotive was shedded at Coniston. There were not as many excursions as might have been expected on a line of this type but those from Blackpool were usually hauled by Stanier class '5MT' 4-6-0 locomotives; the so called 'Black Fives'. These engines, having delivered their trains to Coniston, had to go to Millom to be turned for the return journey because the turntable at Coniston was too short. A short experiment, in 1954, using AEC diesel units did not prove successful enough for the units to be introduced permanently because they could not easily cope with the gradients. In latter days '3F' class 0-6-0s were brought in for use on the freight services and it is probably one of these that operated the last freight train to run on the line. At the very end there was a touch of irony (some might say a final insult!) in that the locomotives used on the demolition trains were diesels in the form of Metro-Vic Co-Bos.

Chapter Five

Finale

A Postscript

In spite of the comparatively early arrival of the railway, Coniston never assumed the sort of standing achieved by Windermere (or more especially Bowness) or Keswick as a tourist spot. Some would express relief about that. Coniston retains, even today, the feel of a place which caters for the walker or climber rather than the tourist who is seeking something akin to what is provided by seaside resorts on the nearby Lancashire coast. Certainly tourism became very much an issue in the minds of the promoters but the railway was not well placed for those who came from the South, in particular. Carrying out copper ore was a prime consideration in building the line and to extend the system from Broughton was the logical thing to do. If the line had been planned a little later with tourism as a major incentive and once the Ulverston-Lancaster line was well established, it would have made more sense to take the line in a route from the Ulverston & Lancaster Railway along the Crake Valley. Such a line would have given better access and avoided the journey round the West Coast of (what is now) Cumbria. So here there was something of a 'Catch 22' situation and one which resulted in the Coniston branch being the earliest significant closure in the rail network of the area. Then again the coming of the Coniston branch was not really heralded as a major event. There was no ceremony to cut the first sod and no grand opening with the associated junketing and celebrations; it just happened. Even so, there are many who visited (and possibly still do visit) Coniston who have fond memories of this little branch, transporting them, as it did, to a very special area of the Lake District.

The Present

Some evidence of the Coniston Railway still remains (2006) although much of the line and its buildings have disappeared. The impressive station at Coniston has gone, and the site has been overbuilt. Broughton station is a private dwelling, as is Torver station, where the old goods shed can also be seen next to a section of the road which has been widened. Woodland station is now two private dwellings. Little evidence of the line remains in Broughton. Some of the bridges can still be seen. What is very encouraging is a scheme to improve the footpath facilities on some sections of the old trackbed in rather the same way as has been done on the trackbed of the former Cockermouth, Keswick & Penrith Railway.

The arch of the footbridge at Coniston has survived. In 1964 it was purchased by Patrick Satow, who was Chairman of the Ravenglass & Eskdale Railway at the time. He donated it to the railway and it arrived at Ravenglass in November.

This photograph of Coniston station was taken from the engine shed, shortly after the closure of the line.
Keith Burgess

Lifting of the track was in progress when this photograph was taken. The location is about one mile south-west of Torver. It is a weekend and the sleeper has been fixed across the end of the rails because work was discontinued during weekends.   *Keith Burgess*

The platforms at Woodland station on 29th July, 1987.   *RCTS Collection*

The crane in the goods shed at Torver on 29th July, 1987.

RCTS Collection

The dilipidated goods shed at Torver on 29th July, 1987. *RCTS Collection*

The station site at Coniston on 1st October, 1997. *Warwick Burton*

By the Spring of 1966 it had been put in place and until January 2004 it stood at the west end of the station at Ravenglass. It was a popular place for watching the trains arriving from Eskdale. In January 2004 it was taken out of this position in order to open up the station area. Whatever its next site, it will be preserved for posterity.

... and Finally

A trip on the rebuilt *Gondola*, coupled with the use of a little imagination, might well transport the traveller to a bygone era (the scenery is much the same!) and for a short time the past can be rolled into the present and a taste of those halcyon days savoured with the relish of the smell of steam!

The footbridge at Coniston was saved for posterity when Patrick Satow purchased it in the 1960s and donated it to the Ravenglass & Eskdale Railway. It is seen here installed at Ravenglass station where it stood until January 2004.   *Author*

Appendix One

Chronology

1845   Three schemes to link the Lancaster & Carlisle and the North Western Railway to the Furness. One includes a link along the Crake Valley to Coniston. All fail. Extensions of Furness Railway planned from Crooklands to Ulverston and Kirkby to Broughton.

1846   Furness Railway has conveyances from Kirkby to Coniston.

1848   12th December. Furness Railway agrees to spend £500 improving the road from Broughton to Coniston.
Agrees to carry copper for not more than 3s. 6d. per ton.

1849   17th December. Notice appears in the *Ulverston Advertiser* relating to the proposal to build 'The Broughton and Coniston Railway'. This was a proposal to build a narrow gauge line (3 ft 3 in.) from Broughton to Coniston. No significant documentary evidence for this appears to have survived. The scheme was not implemented.

1850   1st November. The Whitehaven & Furness Junction Railway opens its last section of the line to a junction with the Furness Railway near Foxfield. It obtains running powers over the Furness Railway to Broughton. Broughton becomes the terminus for the two railways.

1856   20th November. Notice appears in the *Ulverston Advertiser* of a scheme to build 'The Coniston Railway'.

1857   Coniston Railway Company proposes a line from Broughton to Coniston.
10th August. Act (20 & 21 Vict. cap. 110).
17th November. Child & Pickles awarded the contract to build the line.

1859   25th February. Announced that contractors have gone bankrupt.
25th May. Colonel Yolland inspects the line but does not approve it for opening.
14th June. Further inspection. Opening of line approved with certain provisos.
18th June. Line opened for passenger traffic.
30th November. Steam vessel *Gondola* launched.

1860   Extension to copper mines wharf.

1861   Fatal accident.

1862   7th July. Act by which Coniston Railway becomes part of the Furness Railway.

1897   May. Tyer's Electric Tablet System introduced.

1898   Report by Colonel Yorke.

1905   Rail motor commences service on the line

1908   Steam Yacht *Lady of the Lake* enters service.

1923   Line becomes part of the London Midland & Scottish Railway.

1948   Line becomes part of British Railways following the nationalisation of the railways.

1958   Passenger services withdrawn. Last train on 4th October.

1961   Enthusiasts' special. Last significant working.

1962   April. Freight services withdrawn. Line closed completely.

1963   Track removed.

Timetable of *Gondola* Sailings, 1895 and 2006

Timetable of 'Gondola' Sailings for July 1895

Daily, except Sundays		am	pm	pm	pm
Waterhead	depart	11.10	12.45	2.10	4.10
Lake Bank	arrive	11.45	1.20	2.45	4.45
	depart	11.50	1.25	2.50	4.50
Waterhead	arrive	12.25	2.00	3.25	5.25

Special Tours of the Lake at 9.50 am from Waterhead when required.
And on Saturday at 5.30, returning from Lake Bank at 6.10.

Timetable of 'Gondola' Sailings for 1st April to 31st October, 2006

Sundays to Fridays		am	pm	pm	pm	pm
Coniston Pier	depart	11.00	12.00	2.00	3.00	4.00
Brantwood	depart	11.35	12.35	2.35	3.35	4.35
Coniston Pier	arrive	11.45	12.45	2.45	3.45	4.45

Saturdays only		am	pm	pm	pm	pm
Coniston Pier	depart	11.00	12.00	2.00	3.00	4.00
Brantwood	depart	11.25	12.25	2.25	3.35	4.35
Monk Coniston	depart	11.35	12.35	2.35	3.35	4.35
Coniston Pier	arrive	11.45	12.45	2.45	3.45	4.45

Round Trip: Adult, £5.90; Child (aged 2-15), £2.90.
Family Ticket: Two adults and four children (aged 2-15), £14.50.
Children under two years of age sail free of charge.

Sources and Acknowledgements

Deposited Plans, Bills and Acts of Parliament
Directors' Minutes
  Coniston Railway Company
  Furness Railway Company
Shareholders Minutes
Local Newspapers
  Soulby's Ulverston Advertiser
  Barrow News
  Barrow Herald
  Evening Mail
  Lancaster Guardian
  Westmorland Gazette
  Illustrated London News
Timetables
  Furness Railway
  London Midland & Scottish Railway
  British Railways
National Railway Museum Archive
The Copper Development Association

Locations

The National Archive, Kew (formerly the Public Record Office)
The House of Lords Record Office
The British Library
The British Library National Newspaper Archive, Colindale
Barrow Library
Kendal Library
Lancaster Library
The Staffordshire Record Office

Thanks

Substantial amounts of source material for the Coniston Railway proved hard to find. It was not a railway with a high profile in spite of serving one of the most beautiful areas of England. I am grateful to all those who provided me with 'leads' for the best places to look and those members of staff of the various records offices and libraries I visited who gave me help and advice. I am also indebted to a number of people who supplied me with information relating to their own experiences (or experiences of those whom they have known) of the line, including Mr Keith Burgess. In addition, I am grateful to Mr Sawyer, of Bembridge, for putting me in touch with Dr Dearden an Old Bembridgean (and also living in Bembridge) for the information relating to John Ruskin and Edward Woolgar and also the relocation of Bembridge School to Coniston.

The Coniston Railway … *finitus cum decore*

Index